Cathedrals for the Curious:

An Introduction to Cathedrals, Minsters and Abbeys in Britain.

Cathedrals for the Curious:

An Introduction to Cathedrals, Minsters and Abbeys in Britain.

Geoffrey Lord

Published by Cathedral Choice

A CIP catalogue record for this book is available from the British Library.

ISBN 978-0-9570445-0-0

Book and cover design by Clare Brayshaw

The photograph on the Front Cover is York Minster
That on the Rear Cover is of a Roof Boss at Southwark Cathedral, London.

Prepared and printed by:

York Publishing Services Ltd
64 Hallfield Road
Layerthorpe
York YO31 7ZQ

Tel: 01904 431213

Website: www.yps-publishing.co.uk

CONTENTS

ACKNOWLEDGEMENTS

I wish to express my thanks to my wife, Jean, for her unflagging support, encouragement, and patience in the tour of all the Cathedrals; my friends Susan Shedden, Jennie Young, and the Reverend William Mounsey for initial proof-reading and advice; the many Deans and Stewards at the Cathedrals, Minsters and Abbeys for their interest and advice, and particularly assistance with photographs. I am conscious of copyright restrictions on photographs at many historic buildings, and wish to thank all concerned for their permission to obtain photographs, and my friend, Eric Bryant, for certain photographs in Wales.

I wish also to thank David Ross, Editor of 'Britain Express' (www.britainexpress.com) who was encouraging and kind in allowing me to use his article on 'Medieval Architecture', and also Alistair Hodge of 'Carnegie Publishing' for use of the article by former Poet Laureate, John Masefield.

Clare Brayshaw, Paula Charles, Cathi Poole and colleagues of York Publishing Services assisted me with skilled advice and assistance for which I am most grateful.

ABOUT THE AUTHOR

The author, Geoffrey Lord, was born in Rochdale. He and his wife Jean have a daughter, Karen and a son, Andrew who are married each with two children. Geoffrey Lord enjoyed a career in Banking, then in the Probation and After-Care Service in South East Lancashire and in Greater Manchester, and finally from 1977 to 1993 as Secretary and Treasurer to the philanthropic Foundation, the Carnegie United Kingdom Trust. He was Founder of 'Artlink Edinburgh and the Lothians' that provides arts activities in community homes and in hospitals, and escorted access for disabled people to arts venues, and in 1981 produced '*The Arts and Disabilities – a creative response to social handicap'* published by Macdonald Publishers. He established the 'Carnegie Inquiry into Arts and Disabled People' that reported in 1985 and the follow-up 'Carnegie Council Review' that reported in 1988, and as a result was Founder of 'The ADAPT Trust' that raised substantial funds and assisted access to all main arts and heritage venues in the UK, closing in 2006 with its 'Mission Accomplished'. He is co-author with architect C. Wycliffe Noble of '*Access for Disabled People to Arts Premises*', published in 2004 by Elsevier Architectural Press. On behalf of the Scottish Government he established in 1981 the 'Unemployed Voluntary Action Fund', initially being Secretary then Chairman of the new charitable Trust, that now operates in Scotland as 'The Voluntary Action Fund'. In 1987-1989, on behalf of the Carnegie Trustees, he arranged a study into the Amateur Arts and then created the 'Voluntary Arts Network' in the UK that supports the amateur in arts and crafts.

Just prior to retirement he established in 1990 the 'Carnegie Inquiry into the Third Age' that reported and became a Carnegie Programme from 1993. He was a member of the initial Lottery Committee for the Scottish Arts Council.

An Honorary Fellowship was conferred upon him by the Manchester Metropolitan University in 1987 for his contribution to Heritage Interpretation and he was made OBE in June 1989 for services to charity. Geoffrey Lord is currently a Trustee of the 'National Youth Orchestras of Scotland', the 'Edinburgh Voluntary Organisations Trust', the 'Murrayfield Dementia Project', and of FIOP 'Faith in Older People Trust'. He is also a Trustee/Director of the company, BSS plc. He is a member of the Church of the Good Shepherd, Edinburgh, and also attends occasionally the St. Mary's Episcopal Cathedral. Geoffrey and his wife, Jean, have just completed a tour of all Cathedrals, Minsters and active Abbeys in Britain. He would describe himself as curious, inquisitive and eager to learn.

PROLOGUE

Many people who visit cathedrals, minsters and abbeys, and even churches, are not only overwhelmed by the surroundings and the glory of the building, but are confused and perhaps embarrassed by the fact that they face a sudden lack of knowledge and understanding of the 'technicalities' that emerge. Titles such as Early English, Romanesque, Gothic or Goth, Perpendicular, and other descriptions in the building such as arcading, bosses, carrels, chantry, consistory court, frescoes, pulpitum, quire, reredos and shrines, and even canons, deans, rectors and liturgy tax the brain and knowledge and can leave one feeling rather insecure and even inferior. That is the last thing that a cathedral or other church should instil. Even a friendly, welcoming steward offering a free and usually excellent leaflet as an aid may not dispel the tension.

Roof bosses, (one of the attractions in a cathedral) have a practical as well as a decorative function. A boss such as this at Norwich Cathedral is a keystone which holds all the stone ribs of the ceiling in place.

It is believed that many of the visitors, as distinct from those attending one of the services, are not Christian or at least not actively Christian, and often do not want a guided tour. Several are tourists from abroad and may never have entered a British cathedral or church. They are curious – eager to learn. Therefore, anything that helps them to understand better the background to their visit is of benefit, especially if information is read prior to another visit, and particularly if the visit encourages them to attend a service, or stay longer to understand and to benefit from their experience.

Cathedrals should inspire, not just instil.

The Volunteer Guides are usually warm in their welcome, particularly if a visitor joins in a tour with an experienced Guide. Cathedrals, abbeys, minsters and churches are generally free to enter, especially for prayer and worship, but it should be explained that some cathedrals, especially those welcoming tourists daily, make a charge of a 'voluntary donation' to offset the massive costs of maintenance, while others still retain their free entry and trust that donations will be forthcoming.

Cathedrals usually have a poster at entry indicating how much it costs daily to manage a cathedral: it is a high cost and challenging task for those who manage the historic building, even without considering the cost of worship in the services.

All 'donations', especially at services, can be 'Gift-Aided' if the contributor from Britain pays tax to Inland Revenue, so that the cathedral can reclaim a portion of tax and improve its income, and the individual donor can reduce the cost of the donation – a government gift with taxpayers' money!

It should be emphasised also to all visitors that the abbey, cathedral, chapel, church or minster is primarily a place of worship, but it is mainly the beauty, history and mystique of such a building that attracts and inspires a visitor, and challenges one's curiosity.

PREFACE

What then is a cathedral and what should it do?

A former Poet Laureate, John Masefield, who had links with the Liverpool Anglican Cathedral, had this to say in an address to colleagues at lunch after a culminating service for the foundation of dean and chapter at Liverpool Anglican Cathedral on Sunday 4th October 1931. *(The text is reprinted by kind permission of the publisher, Carnegie Publishing 1991, as listed in 'Further Reading').*

"To most of us a Cathedral is a big and beautiful building, made from four to seven centuries ago by men of extraordinary genius, as an offering to God, and as a house for the throne from which the bishop might watch them draw near. Usually such a building is kept in good repair, it is often thronged with sightseers, who sometimes in the course of a year contribute large sums towards its upkeep. Sometimes the sightseer is slightly inconvenienced by the presence of a few old men and women, gathered in a corner to listen while a man in vestments gabbles something, but the inconvenience comes seldom and is always slight. The sightseer is usually more pestered by guides, who will tell him that such an arch is late 13th century and the other window is early 14th, and expect money payment for the information.

Looking into his guide book, he will read that Ruskin thought such a tracery was the last quite pure tracery to be traced by an upright heart, and that somebody else thought that the profound knowledge evident in every line of the bishop's tomb marks the culminating point of the Cinquecento *(500: a term used to describe the Italian Renaissance of the 16th century, including the current styles of architecture).*

Coming away from such a place, the sightseer sometimes reflects that the place is dead and had better be buried. As it happens I have only once, and then for only two weeks, lived sufficiently near to any cathedral to have felt its influence in my life. Cities today have become too big for the citizens to have a civic sense; a city dweller may well be five miles from his Cathedral: so it has happened to myself. Often a city dweller cannot see his Cathedral without making a special journey.

This brings me to my first point of what a cathedral should be. It should be, first of all, a place plainly to be seen by the citizens, and by those in the district. The Parthenon at Athens is the most perfectly placed of all great temples. The sites of many castles would be perfect for cathedrals. Amiens is well-placed, so is Durham; so are York, Gloucester, Salisbury and St. Paul's Cathedral. So is this great Cathedral of Liverpool. A Liverpool Cathedral should be readily seen from many points of the city, and above all, by the life of the city, the river, with its ships and docks. All Cathedrals should be specially conspicuous by tower or spire, and these again should be made more conspicuous by some great figure of white or gold, the guardian of the city; and some further glory of wind-vanes telling the wind-shifts, and great bells telling the hours and their quarters, and ringing for the city's joy: in this city for the ship launched or the ship come home. And in this city I would have the tower such that mariners, who are the life of the city, could adjust their compasses by it, and see the storm signals and the time signals upon it, so that it should be their tower pre-eminently. Then Cathedrals have been made great in the past because their citizens have believed in them, and have given greatly of their best to make them glorious. In their great times they have provided for all great artists the opportunity to indulge the imagination to the full. They have used the best skill of their time. The skill in a nation does not vary greatly from century to century, but in some centuries it is encouraged, and greatly used, in others it is neglected. In others it is depressed and abused. Cathedrals in the past have taken the very best skill of their time and encouraged it to the full. Their builders, sculptors and painters, their metal workers, paviors, glaziers and carpenters have been of their best. All the skilled ones of the time have had the joy of contributing; and the rich ones have had the joy of helping. Poets, perhaps, have been looked at somewhat askance by Cathedrals in the past (I do not here blame the Cathedrals wholly) and the results of their coolness may be seen in the hymnals. Still, some of the noblest Cathedrals' decorations known to me are illustrations of Dante; and there was a time when at York and at Coventry, if not elsewhere, poets gave of their best to link the life of the city with the city's holiest place.

Certainly a Cathedral, besides being visible at a distance, should be splendid within, with the best that all artists and citizens can offer. This splendour should touch and mark all her parts and precincts, and not only her building, but the many institutions attached to her, for teaching, healing and relieving. She should be the place to which all the generalities of her citizens, as well of those of the artists of the time, should turn and flow.

Then since the main purpose of a Cathedral is worship, and the Dedication of a Cathedral is to some special attribute of what is ever to be worshipped; that Dedication should have its Feast of a solemnity great and touching, in some way that many might share and all feel. Here the arts are needed, for by the arts men are linked, as by intellect men are kept asunder. How the touching of all souls may be wrought, is for inspiration to show, but no Cathedral can be serving life that does not draw Life into it, all the Life of its community. Sports, contests, exhibitions, draw whole communities; they always did and always will; contest and spectacle cannot fail. Yet they have always yielded their place as chief attraction to the sincerity of men in earnest.

This Cathedral of Liverpool, the greatest of modern Cathedrals, is a Church of the Resurrection. It comes into the life of our time, in a decade when all the ways of life known to us from childhood have to be remade, when the nation has to be recreated, with what difficulty we do not yet know, but no doubt with much. This Cathedral, therefore, should be the symbol of that Resurrection; and at the same time its standard. What has been muffled and in shrouds and buried deep down after being broken by the soldiers, should emerge here and be triumphant. **Then indeed it would be a Cathedral that Is and Is as it should be**." John Masefield.

With 'tongue in cheek' the then Poet Laureate extols the many virtues and problems of a cathedral. Certainly, a cathedral should be a place to be seen, great, and encouraging the best of skills, splendid within and the place to which citizens should turn and flow. However, not one of the cathedrals in Britain now gives the impression "that it is dead and had better be buried". In fact, quite the opposite, so that may indicate progress over the past 80 years, which is encouraging and contrary to much of the bad news about churches in general.

ONE

Nothing is straightforward in the world of cathedrals and churches, but certainly much is historic and occasionally romantic. It is often thought that the cathedral is a church presided over by a bishop, but not so. The Greek word 'kathedra' leading to the Latin word 'cathedra' means a 'seat': the word came to mean the bishop's seat or throne (originally the chair of a teacher – rather than the throne of a monarch). So a cathedral is the important church in a diocese; one of the regions of the church (Anglican, Roman Catholic or of an Orthodox Church) that contains the bishop's throne or seat.

A cathedral is sometimes called the 'mother church', as with Canterbury Cathedral as the mother church of the Anglican Communion, and Westminster Cathedral as the Roman Catholic Mother Church. Similarly, it is often thought that all cities have a cathedral. That is not the case, Cambridge and Nottingham being two exceptions, although most cathedrals are located in a city or near to one; for example, at Ely near to Cambridge, and at Southwell near to Nottingham. In South Wales the cathedral is located in the small village of Llandaff near Cardiff. There is the famous St. David's Cathedral (shown overleaf) in the smallest town in Wales – St. David's – built on the site of a 6th century monastery.

St. David's Cathedral, Wales

In Scotland the Episcopal Church (Anglican) has eight cathedrals; and the Church of Scotland, that is Presbyterian without bishops, has nine churches still called cathedrals for historical reasons, such as St. Giles Cathedral in Edinburgh. Its Glasgow Cathedral is said to be the largest church to have survived the 16th century Reformation and has the finest collection of post-war stained glass in Britain. Apart from wars, such as the Civil War that caused much damage to cathedrals and abbeys, it was probably the Reformation in the reign of Henry VIII that caused the utmost revolution and damage to abbeys and cathedrals.

A concise account of this period is given in Appendix D.

St. Patrick's Anglican Cathedral

In Northern Ireland the Church of Ireland (Anglican) has eight cathedrals and the Roman Catholic Church three cathedrals. In Armagh is the Anglican St. Patrick's Cathedral, and here also is the Roman Catholic St. Patrick's Cathedral. Some of the dioceses overlap between the North and the Republic of Ireland and just to

St. Patrick's R.C. Cathedral, Armagh

confuse further, there is more than one cathedral to a diocese – several churches named as cathedrals in Northern Ireland are in essence parish churches. There is special history here: St. Columb's Cathedral in Londonderry is the city's oldest building from 1633 and this was the first cathedral to have

been built in Britain after the Reformation – in the city founded by the Saint in the 6th century. In this troubled city, the cathedral is a landmark for the promotion of ecumenical activities. St. Peter's RC Cathedral in Belfast is the first Catholic church to have been built in the

St. Columb's Cathedral Londonderry

Gothic Revival style, without transepts, in Scrabo sandstone with Scottish sandstone dressings, apparently inspired by famous architect AWN Pugin, and recently restored with further stone from Scotland. St. Anne's Anglican Cathedral in Belfast is the only cathedral to have two bishop's seats (see later under 'cathedra'). St. Patrick's RC Cathedral in Armagh has a peculiar reputation; an important building that changed architect and architectural style halfway up the walls: the bottom half designed in 1838 in English Perpendicular style and the top half designed in 1853 in French decorated style: a ravishing product.

Even more importantly, outside of Rome – known as the Holy See – Armagh is the oldest Episcopal See (the See is similar to a diocese and the seat of the bishop) in the world. Ireland's patron saint – Patrick – is buried above beautiful Strangford Lough in Downpatrick, at the site of a monastery besides Down Anglican Cathedral dating from the 12th century, and a place of pilgrimage, especially on the 17th March – the date now accepted from 1607 as the date of his death probably in 461AD. Naturally, the town of Downpatrick has a fine St. Patrick's Centre describing the saint's life and travels.

Abbeys, some active but most as historic ruins, are generally located in or near a town with a significant history, except of course for the famous Westminster Abbey (known as a 'Royal Peculiar') in the heart of London. The town of Beverley in England has its minster, and has two parish churches, the Minster and St. Mary's. However, York Minster is in a city and is the cathedral for the diocese. Confusing? Perhaps, but challenging! It is a complicated history and tradition, but also flexible and some might say 'truly in the style of the Church'.

A list of all cathedrals with contact details is in Appendix A.

The cathedrals, minsters and abbeys of England are usually open daily to visitors, although in the other countries, as in Northern Ireland, smaller cathedrals may not be open each day, and as with the Episcopal cathedral in Glasgow may be closed on several days, not being in the centre of the city and due to lack of staff. Surprisingly, the Roman Catholic cathedral in the heart of Sheffield is closed on Sunday afternoons to 'avoid damage'. There is usually also one church, such as a parish church in a town or in a district of a city, that is open to visitors, but unfortunately most other churches are now closed except at times of services, especially in towns and cities other than in tourist areas due to the risk of vandalism and theft. Usually there is a contact name displayed at a church so that one can make an arrangement for a visit other than at times of a service.

In these days of the world-wide web, typing in the name of an abbey, cathedral or church will

Fountains Abbey
Furness Abbey at Barrow in Furness was one of the richest Cistercian monasteries in England, exceeded only by Fountains Abbey at Ripon in Yorkshire.

Furness Abbey

usually display several excellent sites that detail history, activities and opening times, often with a 'virtual tour'. Interestingly, the BBC has a website called 'Seven Man-Made Wonders' which covers various regions of England and includes the following cathedrals as exceptional: Canterbury, Chichester, Durham, Ely, Exeter, Hereford, Lincoln, London St. Paul's, plus Fountains Abbey and Furness Abbey. In Scotland, there is the excellent publication, now in three volumes, describing most churches in Scotland with details for visitors: Sacred Edinburgh & Midlothian, Sacred Fife and the Forth Valley, & Sacred South West Scotland, with information on its website: www.sacredscotland.org.uk.

This **'Introduction to Cathedrals'** attempts, therefore, to assist those of us who are curious and to explain some of the mysteries of the 'technical' so that forewarned is forearmed in the hope that the cathedral – or minster, abbey or church – becomes a warm, exciting experience. Having visited and experienced the building and its artefacts – a product of human art and workmanship – the next stage is to experience more of the human element through the services. Try Choral Evensong in an Anglican/Episcopal cathedral, or Sung Vespers in a Catholic cathedral, with its outstanding liturgy – a form of public worship almost daily. If possible sit in the quire (or choir) – a significant part of the chancel of a cathedral and minster – and listen to choir and clergy sing this act of worship – a thing of beauty. If this is too challenging, then just enjoy the building, its artefacts and history, and understand the dedication, sacrifice and skill that has created the whole of the historic building.

We should remember though, that the church is not a museum and not only a building: it is the Christians who witness there!

TWO

THE CATHEDRAL is a church containing a 'cathedra' – the chair (or throne) of a bishop, and is the principal church of a diocese (a district under the pastoral care of a bishop). Initially, any church that served as the primary location of a bishop was considered his seat, or cathedral, and was therefore known as a cathedral.

There are 25 medieval cathedral buildings in England dating from between 1040 and 1540 that, as buildings, constitute a major part of the artistic heritage of Britain and are major symbols of Christianity. They are distinctly English and yet have great diversity one to another and indeed within each building. Part of the challenge and charm is to find the various phases of the building, such as at Hereford, that alone has an aspect of each main part of architectural heritage. At Worcester that demonstrates every style from Norman to Perpendicular, or at Salisbury where 'stylistic unity' is said to be demonstrated because the cathedral was built within a very short time-scale, 1200-1275 in Early English style, apart from the 14th century tower and spire. Winchester is said to be the longest medieval cathedral in the world.

The following 25 are thought to have commenced, in the building of the new 'cathedral', on the following dates:

Ripon 9-10th century, Lincoln 1074, St. Albans 1077, Hereford 1079, Winchester 1079, Worcester 1084, Chichester 1088, Ely 1090, Carlisle 1092, Durham 1093, Chester 1093, Norwich 1096, Gloucester 1098, Southwell 1108, Exeter 1112, Peterborough 1117, Bristol 1140, York 1154, Oxford 1158, Canterbury 1172, Wells 1175, Rochester 1177, Lichfield 1195, Southwark 1208, Salisbury 1220 – all built over several centuries.

In addition, London 'Old St. Pauls' (fourth in architectural history) was 11th century, the new (fifth) St. Paul's is from 1675; and Westminster Abbey was a previous cathedral from 1541 until 1641.

It is important to remember that all the medieval buildings, now cathedrals, were originally Roman Catholic as they came before the Reformation in 1536, but now are part of the Church of England as the result of the change of the official religion of the country that occurred in the reign of Henry VIII in 1534.

To complicate matters further, the dates of dioceses and their cathedrals are different. Beginning in 597 when St. Augustine set up his monastery at Canterbury until Carlisle in 1133, there are recorded 17 dioceses and cathedrals from the 6-12th centuries:

Canterbury 597, Rochester 604, St. Paul's London 604, York 625, Winchester 660, Lichfield 669, Hereford 676, Worcester 680, Wells 909, Durham 990, Exeter 1050, Lincoln 1072, Chichester 1075, Salisbury 1078, Norwich 1091, Ely 1109, Carlisle 1133.

Then five dioceses and cathedrals founded by Henry VIII, the first for 400 years all in 1541:

Bristol, Chester, Gloucester, Oxford Christ Church, Peterborough, (and also Westminster – its cathedral status withdrawn in 1641).

The first 22 listed are ancient cathedrals of medieval status in the Church of England.

Then 20 dioceses and cathedrals founded in the 19th & 20th centuries; the first at Ripon in 1836.

Ripon 1836*, Manchester (PC) 1848, St. Albans 1877*, Truro 1877, Liverpool 1880, Newcastle (PC) 1882, Southwell 1884*, Wakefield (PC) 1888, Birmingham (PC) 1905, Southwark 1905*, Chelmsford (PC) 1914, St. Edmundsbury (PC)1914, Sheffield (PC) 1914, Coventry 1918 (rebuilt 1962), Bradford (PC) 1919, Blackburn (PC) 1926, Derby (PC) 1927, Guildford 1927, Leicester (PC) 1927, Portsmouth (PC) 1927.

The four later cathedrals with a star*(Ripon, St. Albans, Southwell and Southwark) are ancient churches that have not previously had cathedral status. Twelve with a (PC) were of parish church status attaining cathedral status more recently. Truro, Liverpool, Coventry and Guildford are newly built. See more detail later. The last cathedral appears to have been established in 1927.

The appointment of bishops spread into Britain from early times of Christianity, with the earliest surviving diocesan system in Wales from the 6th century, where there are now six cathedrals of the Church in Wales (Anglican). Only four are medieval and one, St. David's, occupies special status and is known as the *'Welsh Westminster Abbey'*. Bangor was founded in 525, the second cathedral in Britain, although nothing remains of that structure (the cathedral has had a chequered career: a 12th century Norman church was destroyed by Edward I during his conquest of Wales; nothing remains of the rebuild from 1291 burned down again during a rebellion in 1404: the nave and tower are early Tudor).

St. Asaph in North Wales is said to be the smallest cathedral in Britain. Dating from AD560, the existing building is largely 14th century and was remodelled by Sir Gilbert Scott in 1867-75.

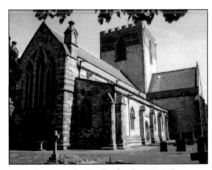

St. Asaph Cathedral. N Wales.

Irish dioceses appear to have been established mainly in the Viking period, and in Northern Ireland there are eight cathedrals of the Church of Ireland that also has five cathedrals in the Republic.

In Scotland medieval dioceses were based on a 12th century structure but some had earlier roots, for example at Galloway founded by St. Ninian c.400. The situation in Scotland now is very different: The Church of Scotland is Presbyterian in structure and does not, strictly speaking, have cathedrals because it does not have bishops, but is governed by Kirk Sessions at parish level, Presbyteries at regional level and ultimately by its highest court, 'The General Assembly' which meets annually and elects a moderator for each year.

The crown steeple of St. Giles' cathedral in Edinburgh dates from the 15th century

Its cathedrals in Scotland became redundant when bishoprics were abolished: some were abandoned, some destroyed; others became parish churches. However, there are still nine cathedrals in name, for example St. Giles of Edinburgh that lies on the Royal Mile. Despite its name, St. Giles' Cathedral was only a cathedral for two short periods when bishops served in the Scottish Church, from 1633-38 and from 1661-89.

The Scottish Episcopal Church in the 18th century was 'Jacobite' in allegiance, loyal to the House of Stuart. Following the failure of the 1745 Jacobite Rebellion the Episcopal Church was suppressed under penal laws and its cathedrals made forfeit. The present-day eight cathedrals of the Scottish Episcopal Church were all built in the 19th century after the partial repeal of the penal laws.

Amazingly, in England 11 of the Saxon dioceses survive. A rising population had required a better organisation so that 20 Anglican dioceses were created since 1836 and large parish churches were converted into cathedrals.

A few ambitious dioceses – Guildford, Liverpool and Truro – built new cathedrals. The modern cathedral at Coventry was built after the destruction of its parish church cathedral in World War II. There are now 44 dioceses of the Church of England with 42 cathedrals in England, one in the Isle of Sodor and Man, and one in Gibraltar for Europe. The Anglican 'Mother' Cathedral, Canterbury, is the first cathedral founded in England and has a tremendous history. Canterbury Cathedral houses the cathedra of the Archbishop of Canterbury, the Chair of St. Augustine, although his official residence is Lambeth Palace in London. England belonged to the Western (Catholic) Church for almost a thousand years, from the time of Augustine of Canterbury; but in 1534, during the reign of King Henry VIII, the Catholic Church in England was separated from the broader Catholic Church, when a new Church of England was created with Henry as its 'supreme governor'. Under his son, Edward VI, the Church of England became more influenced by the European Protestant movement but rejoined the Roman Catholic Church during the reign of Queen Mary I in 1555. Two 'Statutes of Repeal' to mark the reunion with Roman Catholicism were created but the reunion was short-lived. Mary's sister, Elizabeth I, came to the throne in 1558, re-established independence from Rome in a 1559 settlement and was finally excommunicated in 1570. Roman Catholicism continued in England, although it was subject to various forms of persecution, with most members going underground for all practical purposes until 1832 when the Catholic Emancipation Act came into force. Catholic dioceses were re-established in 1850 and gave the opportunity for architects to design new cathedrals. The first was St. Chad's in Birmingham, designed by Augustus Pugin in Gothic Revival style, and it became the standard for new Roman Catholic churches and cathedrals.

However, Liverpool and Bristol produced outstandingly modern RC cathedrals, and the London Westminster Cathedral was built in Byzantine style. Westminster RC Cathedral, not to be confused with the Anglican Westminster Abbey, is the Roman Catholic 'Mother' Cathedral described by Sir John Betjeman as:

"J F Bentley's basilican cathedral is a series of surprises. First, when near to it, you notice the fine quality of the brickwork contrasting with the proportional bands of Portland stone. Everywhere the external detail is precise and delicate, the grouping of turrets, entrances and windows and blank spaces is carefully contrived and never dull, never fussy... From the outside you do not expect what is the greatest surprise of all, that the Cathedral looks larger inside than it looks from the outside."

The Roman Catholic Church has now 21 cathedrals in England, three in Northern Ireland, seven in Scotland and three in Wales, as listed in Appendix A.

In the Middle Ages, cathedrals were not only places of worship, but tools of instruction; their stained glass windows and interior carvings told stories from the bible or represented biblical figures. Cathedrals were designed to inspire awe in the Christians who worshipped there: it seems clear that the Gothic architecture from the Middle Ages achieved this. The construction was a major undertaking that provided employment for local workers and improved the economy of the city and neighbouring towns. Cathedrals had special holiday Masses that attracted worshippers from the surrounding churches, and some sheltered the relics of saints and were therefore sites of pilgrimage.

The respect for Saints was an important aspect of the practice of medieval Christianity and the possession of the relics of a popular saint was a boon to the church. For example, Saint Alban's Abbey contained the relics of England's first Christian martyr; Ripon had the shrine of its founder St. Wilfred; Durham was built to house the bodies of St. Cuthbert of Lindisfarne and St. Aidan; Ely had the shrine of St. Ethelreda; Chichester the remains of St. Richard; and Westminster Abbey the shrine of its founder St. Edward the Confessor. In the 13th century, Canterbury was the main place of pilgrimage (after its conversion to Christianity in 597, St. Augustine became the first Archbishop of Canterbury but Thomas Becket's murder at the cathedral in 1170 led to the cathedral becoming a place of pilgrimage for Christians world-wide. This pilgrimage provided the theme for Chaucer's 14th century literary classic the 'Canterbury Tales').

In Scotland, Dunkeld Cathedral is thought to house the relics of Saint Columba: when the first King of Scotland, Kenneth MacAlpin, established his capital at nearby Scone he brought from Iona the relics of the saint, that are now said to be buried under the chancel steps.

Because travellers drawn to cathedrals helped to make the area fairly prosperous, the residents of any large town were usually happy to have a cathedral built there.

Cathedrals then were not quiet reverential places of worship. It is recorded at Lincoln, for example, that the nave and aisle were the spaces for pilgrims to meet, gossip and share news: perhaps that was one of the reasons for the elaborate chancel screens separating the ordinary people from the priests and supportive worshippers in the quire. Cathedrals were also brightly coloured, before much of the decoration and art was destroyed during the Reformation and Civil War, and indeed during the latter strife cathedrals were often used as garrisons, prisons and stables for horses!

It is important to recognise also that the cathedrals of Britain span the millennium – from cathedrals of the 1100s to those built in Liverpool and Coventry, with an amazing series of styles from Early English Gothic to the Renaissance at St. Paul's, and then the Modernism in the '60s, as of Liverpool's RC Cathedral. Recognising that the Church enjoyed enormous power and wealth in the Middle Ages and up to the Reformation, cathedrals are powerful historic symbols of the place of the Church in society.

A list is provided in Appendix A of all Anglican and Roman Catholic cathedrals in Britain, including the modern cathedrals of the 20th century, such as Coventry (built alongside the ruins of the earlier 14th century cathedral destroyed by enemy action in World War II), Guildford (between 1936-1961) and Liverpool (between 1904-1978) and those 15 known as 'Parish Church Cathedrals' that were raised to cathedral status between 1847 and 1927. The existing Presbyterian 'cathedrals' in Scotland are also listed. In 1778 John Wesley built a chapel at City Road, London and today it is often called the 'Cathedral of Methodism' attracting pilgrims from all over the world. The Coptic, Greek, Russian, Serbian and Ukrainian Orthodox Churches also have cathedrals in Britain that are listed in Appendix A.

THE MINSTER is different from a cathedral in that it was originally founded as a missionary church from which priests set out to convert the people of the surrounding area to Christianity. It is the church of a monastery and now the name given to some important churches – such as Beverley Minster that is not designated as a cathedral but is, unusually, one of two parish churches in that town, and York Minster that acts as a cathedral.

(The original church of York Minster was founded at the time of King Edwin of Northumbria's baptism by Saint Paulinus. It was then transformed from a humble wooden building into one of the finest and most important Gothic cathedrals in England in 627AD). Kidderminster does not now have a minster but was mentioned in the Domesday Book of 1086 when it may have had a minster church.

Additional minsters have been designated in the 21st century, by adding an honorary title to existing parish churches: including Dewsbury (1994), Sunderland (1998), Rotherham (2004), Stoke (2005), and Newport (2008). The Parish Church of St. John the Baptist in Halifax, West Yorkshire, and St. Andrew's Church in Plymouth were elevated to minster status in November 2009. A church with an unusual title is the Church of St. Mary, Sexburgha on the Isle of Sheppey founded in 664AD and known as the 'Minster Abbey'.

THE ABBEY is a building occupied by monks or nuns governed by an abbot or abbess: a church or house that was once an abbey or part of it. Some cathedrals were monastic foundations and may have retained a few of the buildings, perhaps as ruins. When Henry III came to the English throne in 1217 there were around 680 monasteries in the country, and they owned about a fifth of the country's wealth. Westminster Abbey in London is probably the best-known, now attracting thousands of tourists annually, and it is a peculiar church, not a cathedral, but known as the 'royal peculiar' due to its links with the royal family, and its manner of management.

Active abbeys such as Buckfast and Sherborne still have independent management.

Those abbeys that are ruined, or partially ruined, tend to be in the care of the Heritage Organisation of the country, such as Dunfermline Abbey in Scotland that acts as a parish church in the Presbyterian Church of Scotland, with its old abbey church building administered by Heritage Scotland. In England, Fountains Abbey is Yorkshire's first World Heritage Site and is managed by the National Trust in association with English Heritage.

CHURCH has several meanings. Deriving from the Greek *ekklesia* meaning assembly (latinised as ecclesia, and coming to us through Germanic and old English), church can mean 'local congregation' or 'the building where they meet', 'the whole body of Christian people' or 'the specific denomination to which they belong'.

Said to be the oldest church in Britain, St. Peter's Chapel, Bradwell-on-Sea, was built to mark the spot where St. Cedd landed in 654, on his mission from Lindisfarne to bring light to the 'heathen East Angles'. Using bricks and stone from the ruined Roman Fort of Othona, the Saxons created what was almost a cathedral, 50ft (15.2m) long, 22ft (6.7m) wide and 25ft (7.6m) high. The people of Essex had worshipped here for 600 years or more but so remote was this spot that congregations soon dwindled and the chapel was 'lost'. In 1920, a passing rambler noticed the site, started to excavate and soon realised that he was looking at sacred ground, so St. Peter's Chapel was restored.

However, St. Martin's Church in Canterbury is the oldest church in England still in use. It is a fascinating building with an important history – the starting point of the revival of Christianity in England in 597 AD by St. Augustine. The oldest log church in the world is St. Andrew's Church at Greensted, near Ongar, Essex –although this only really applies now to the walls of the nave, which date from the 11th century. The oldest church door in England, Saxon 1060, is still on St. Botolph's Church in the village of Hadstock in Essex. The oldest working turret, or tower, clock in England is thought to be in the tower of St. Mary's Church in Rye, Sussex.

Said to be the oldest Roman Catholic church in Britain, St. Etheldreda's in London is a stone's throw from the glittering wealth of Hatton Garden, where gold, silver and diamonds are traded: here stands this haven of peace and tranquillity. A hidden ancient gem of the Middle Ages, St. Etheldreda's Church was the town chapel of the Bishops of Ely from about 1250 to 1570. It is one of only two remaining buildings in London from the reign of Edward I and was once one of the most influential places in London with a palace of vast grounds. It was like an independent state, the Bishop of Ely's place in London or Ely Place as it is now called, and its chapel took its name from one of the popular saints of the day, Etheldreda.

CHAPEL has several meanings but a chapel is, mainly, a holy place or area of worship for Christians; sometimes small and attached to a larger institution such as a large church, a college, a hospital, a palace, a prison or a cemetery; sometimes large and unattached to another building. Architecturally, a chapel such as a Lady chapel may be a part of a large church set aside for some specific use or purpose, as in the Cathedral.

Additionally and importantly, 'chapel' is often the title given by local worshippers to their independent place of worship as in the Methodist Church. The New Room in Bristol – originally built in 1739 – is the oldest Methodist chapel in the world and the beginning of the early Methodist movement. It was built and used by John Wesley and the early Methodists as a meeting and preaching place, and a centre for helping and educating the needy members of the community. The chapel itself is on the ground floor, where there is also a shop, and upstairs are the preachers' rooms where the museum is located, containing a unique collection of papers and artefacts, that tell the story of John and Charles Wesley and their life and work in Bristol.

Note: The following chapters do not cover all technical terms, especially architectural, but only those most likely to arise during a visit.

(Where a technical term such as 'Architrave' is used in a description, as in the entry for 'Abacus', then there is a following explanation under the entry for 'Architrave').

Details of more inclusive guides are in the 'Further Reading' section after the Postscript.

THREE

ABACUS is the load-bearing flat slab or block, of stone or wood, that forms the top of a capital (that is the moulded or carved block on top of a column) as an aid to support the architrave – a main beam above. The abacus, initially in square form, gradually  developed into round forms and with decorative effects of foliage. By the 15th century an abacus had become smaller, like a shelf, and often covered with an excess of 'foliage vegetation'. It is an important feature as it may record the date of its formation.

(Note that an abacus is also the name of the early counting instrument with beads).

The website www.probertencyclopaedia.com explains thoroughly all architectural terms beginning with abacus. A fine website for explanation and photographs of most architectural terms is that of the Corpus of Romanesque Sculpture in Britain and Ireland (King's College London). www.crsbi.ac.uk/resources

AISLE is the passage or open space in a cathedral on either side of the nave from west to east, thus north and south aisles, and separated from the nave by arcades, a row of pillars or columns.

Aisles may stop at the transepts, but often aisles can be continued around the apse (the recess at the east end). Where the aisles continue around a semi-circular quire (choir), thus providing access to a series of chapels, the term is a 'chevet' (just an apsidal end of a church). Aisles are thus categorised as nave-aisles, transept-aisles or choir-aisles.

In Gothic architecture, the roofs of the aisles are lower than that of the nave, allowing light to enter through clerestory windows. Bristol is unusual in that its aisles are the same height as the quire (choir), known as a style of German Gothic 'hall church'. In Romanesque architecture, the roofs are at roughly equal heights, with those of the aisle being only slightly lower than that of the nave.

An early 14ᵗʰC aisle of Bristol Cathedral (see also Arches)

Cathedrals, usually, have only one aisle on each side, with Chichester and Elgin being exceptions with two aisles each side. The walls of the aisles usually house memorials and occasionally have seats in stone in a recess, and often the aisles and its walls have displays about the church and its mission.

In the north aisle of St. Paul's London is a famous statue of the Duke of Wellington, one of Britain's greatest soldiers and statesmen, who died in 1852, with this monument not created until 1912. In the south aisle at Norwich is a skeleton of one Thomas Gooding embedded (or embodied) in the wall: there are also medieval wall paintings in the roof of the aisle. In the north aisle of Winchester Cathedral is a fine font from 1150AD, of Belgian marble and displaying scenes of St. Nicholas. Truro, the first cathedral to be built on a new site since Salisbury in 1220, has a St. Mary's Aisle that was originally part of the parish church and incorporated into the cathedral by the architect.

In the Church of Scotland's Glasgow Cathedral is the Blacader Aisle, probably intended as an undercroft for a chapel above, where the ceiling has fine medieval bosses, and is said to occupy the site of the cemetery consecrated in the 5th century by St. Ninian. Surprisingly, in the south aisle of the Church of Scotland's Dunblane Cathedral is a window depicting England's Patron Saint, St. George, and Hope.

Nearby is a stone memorial commemorating the deaths of schoolchildren in the tragic shooting incident of 1996 at Dunblane Primary School.

In the St. Magnus Cathedral on Orkney are carved reminders of mortality (coffins, hour-glasses, skulls, and other bones) fixed on the walls of each aisle, with the historic writings translated on plaques for the benefit of visitors. Its north aisle contains also a unique wooden grave-marker called a 'mort brod' along with stone grave-markers, relics from outdoor graves.

Aisles can be very historic and interesting, and not just a boring thoroughfare!

ALTAR: described as a flat-top block for offerings to deity, it is the holy table where the Eucharist is celebrated, usually in the chancel, but often now an additional altar is provided in the nave before entry to the quire and chancel.

(It is curious that an additional modern, free-standing altar on a large wooden platform at the London Westminster RC Cathedral has just been removed as "being hideous" and the Mass is now celebrated at the high altar).

In medieval times, an altar may have been erected over the tomb of a saint or even a benefactor. Many are very old and should be viewed for their history. It is recorded that the High Altar at Lichfield Cathedral is over 700 years old. Before the Reformation, Derby had at least six altars, many being statues of saints. After the Reformation, stone altars were generally replaced by wooden communion tables.

A frontal is often placed over the altar – an embroidered cloth in colours that reflect the seasons of the church, although some are embroidered for special occasions, such as in gold and white for weddings.

One of the most magnificent frontals is at Bath Abbey with a festive frontal of green and silver illustrating a fountain of life.

There is usually also a wood or metal altar rail often richly decorated. It is recorded in the 17th century that an archbishop, William Laud, ordered rails to protect the altar from abuse by animals, perhaps when cathedrals were used as markets. It is said that prior to altar rails a cloth was

Derby Cathedral Altar with new frontal

held in front of communicants to prevent crumbs of the consecrated bread falling to the floor.

Worcester Cathedral high altar frontal

At the east end of Durham Cathedral is a finely carved, 14th century Caen stone altar screen that originally contained 107 alabaster figures. Behind this masterpiece of craftsmanship, still resting on the site of the original Saxon shrine, lies the tomb of St. Cuthbert.

Durham Cathedral: High altar screen

AMBULATORY is literally a place for walking or an arcade in an apse or cloister; a covered passage behind the altar usually linking it with chapels at the east end.

APOSTLE comes from the ancient Greek *'apostolos'*. In early Christianity, especially in the biblical *Gospel of Luke*, an apostle was one of the 'Twelve', the inner circle of disciples of Jesus, who were, according to the biblical *Acts of the Apostles* and Christian tradition, disciples whom Jesus of Nazareth had chosen and trained for a specific mission: the 'Great Commission' – the establishment of the Christian Church by evangelism, and the spreading of 'the good news'. The period of early Christianity during the lifetime of the apostles is called the Apostolic Age. In the 2nd century, association with the apostles was evidence of authority and orthodoxy.

Paul's epistles were accepted as scripture, and three of the four gospels were associated with apostles, as were other New Testament works. See also the entry 'disciple' and Appendix C on 'Disciples and Apostles'.

Apostle is used in many forms today: *'The Apostle'* is a 1903 choral work by Edward Elgar; it is also the name of a secret society at Cambridge University. There is now also the broader meaning of a messenger and ambassador: this more general meaning translated into Latin as *'missio'* gives us 'missionary'.

APSE is a large semi-circular or polygonal (usually more than four sides) recess; an arched or domed roof especially at the east end of a building.

In Britain the apse is usually squared, but on the continent rounded apses are common. An unusual apse is that at St. Paul's London that houses the American Memorial Chapel, honouring American servicemen and women who died in World War II, with a roll of honour containing the names of 28,000 who died in service. An apse at the Westminster RC Cathedral contains a major part of

Westminster Cathedral Chapel of the Apostle to the Gentiles, with Apse and Triptych of St. Paul in gilt bronze.

the fine organ there, and another in a chapel has an altar and triptych. (See also photo under triptych).

When completed in the 12th century, the Romanesque St. Magnus Cathedral in Kirkwall, the capital of Orkney, had three aisled bays to the chancel, with one 'apsed' similar to the original apse at Durham and with eight bays to the nave as at Durham and Dunfermline Abbey, probably built by the same craftsmen travelling the islands. Belfast Cathedral has an eastern apse and ambulatory containing books of remembrance.

ARCADE, in a shopping centre, is a passage arched over. In a cathedral it is a row of arches, between the nave and aisles, or between quire (choir) and aisles, supporting the main wall that is pierced by windows in a 'clerestory' (in an aisled building, the part of the main wall that is pierced with windows to give light to the interior).

Winchester (shown here), with the longest nave, has very tall arches in its arcade.

Exeter Cathedral's interior is described as 'an avenue of stately trees with branches interlacing overhead".

ARCADING is thus a series of arches supporting, or along, a wall whose shape varies according to when it was constructed.

As an example, in the semi-ruined Dunkeld Cathedral in its beautiful location in Scotland, the nave was eventually reconstructed in the early part of the 15th century and was a magnificent example of Scottish Gothic architecture. Now a roofless shell, it remains an impressive sight with long arcades of clustered columns supported by massive cylindrical piers along the length of the nave. Sitting above this arrangement is an unusual design of triforium with some sturdy tracery spanning its low, wide arches and, at the highest level, a row of small round-headed windows with flowing tracery forms the clerestory.

Dunkeld Cathedral: Ruins

St. David's Cathedral in Wales was begun between 1180 and 1182 and is the result of centuries of rebuilding: constructed in the Norman style using purple Cambrian sandstone, it has survived both the collapse of its tower and an earthquake in the 13th century, although today the floor slopes noticeably, the arcades veer from the vertical, and the east and west ends of the building vary in height by about four metres.

At Southwark Cathedral in London, the great nave is more modern, but its design blends with the older parts of the building and in the south aisle can be seen some of the 13th century arcading. (Nearby is the modern memorial to the victims of the Marchioness Disaster, when a River Thames pleasure boat sank near to the cathedral. Prior to the memorial being installed this space was occupied by the font, thus the unusual shape of the memorial).

ARCH is a self-supporting arrangement of bricks or stone that carries the weight of a wall over an opening. The width is known as the 'span'; its height is the 'rise'. In English cathedrals, arches are either semi-circular (in Romanesque, Norman or Renaissance periods) or pointed. The history of 'pointed' is that they were thought to have been introduced from the Middle East by experience in the Crusades; first at Durham in the early 12th century, and now considered the 'hallmark' of Gothic architecture. Before the 'Gothic' ended in the 16th century there were several varieties of pointed shape, from lancet or acute arch to equilateral, explained further in chapter five. (See also 'keystone'.)

Bristol Cathedral is said to be one of the finest examples of a 'hall church' with the sense of light and space throughout the building, as a result of its consistent height and its tall, single span arches, unparalleled among other medieval cathedrals.

At St. Albans (overleaf) there are Early English arches from the early 13th century enlargement, and decorated arches from a rebuilding after a partial collapse in 1323.

At Lincoln the only surviving part of the first Norman cathedral is to be seen in the West Front with the three round-headed arches over the doors and the north and south niches, perhaps based on the design of a Roman triumphal arch.

> *"I have always held and proposed against all comers to maintain that the Cathedral of Lincoln is out and out the most precious piece of architecture in the British Isles." – John Ruskin.*

There is one of these arches – scissor structures – on each of three sides of the Crossing at Wells.

Wells Cathedral unique tower crossing

FOUR

ARCHBISHOP, BISHOP, DEAN, PROVOST and DIOCESE: The Anglican Church has two archbishops in England, one of Canterbury, the other of York, both of whom are invested with 'first rank' dignity; and two archbishops in Ireland, one of Armagh, the other of Dublin.

Their authority is similar to that of Catholic archbishops.

In Scotland the Episcopal Church has no archbishop; but one of the bishops is chosen by the rest to act as 'Primus'. The post of Archbishop of Wales was created in 1920 when the Church in Wales was separated from the Church of England (of which the four Welsh dioceses had previously been part); the new Church became the Welsh province of the Anglican Communion. Unlike the Archbishops of Canterbury and York, who are appointed by the Queen upon the advice of the Prime Minister, the Archbishop of Wales is one of the six diocesan Bishops of Wales, elected to hold this office in addition to his own diocese.

In the Roman Catholic Church an archbishop (or metropolitan), is a bishop who governs a diocese strictly his own, while he presides at the same time over the bishops of a well-defined district composed of simple dioceses but not of provinces.

A bishop is an ordained or consecrated member of the Christian clergy generally entrusted with a position of authority and oversight. Both archbishop and bishop play an important role in the life, development and teaching of the respective Churches, but as stated earlier they do not have control of the cathedrals in which there is the bishop's seat. The history, meaning and structure are complicated and reach back to soon after the death of Christ.

DEAN: soon after the Battle of Hastings in 1066, many of the Norman bishops, introduced by and as supporters of William the Conqueror, became involved in Parliament and politics, rising to positions of influence where their duties took them away from their cathedral for which they may have been the inspiration of the building. One result was that the senior canon appointed became the dean with the responsibility of managing the cathedral: he is the chief officer of a chapter; he is an ecclesiastical magistrate next in degree to bishop, and has immediate charge of the cathedral and its estates. However there have been problems in recent times in recruitment and mainly over the difficulty of finances.

One retiring dean has been quoted as: *"Ten years ago the job was very attractive, but it has become exceedingly busy and responsible now and it could involve a great deal of administration. Many clergy just don't want to become involved in that."* But in 2004 Canon June Osborne was installed as the 80th Dean of Salisbury – the first woman dean in the history of this, Britain's finest 13th century cathedral, and the first female dean at any of Britain's medieval cathedrals. She said: *"there is no better job in the Church of England than being dean of a cathedral – and no better cathedral for me than Salisbury."*

The title of provost was given to heads of chapter who were also incumbents with the cure of souls. Therefore in the Church of England, cathedrals which were also parish churches and the new 19th and 20th century cathedrals had provosts until the year 2000 when they were all re-designated as deans. In the Scottish Episcopal Church, the senior priest of a cathedral still holds the title of provost and every diocese has a dean, an appointment equivalent to that of archdeacon in the Church of England.

DIOCESE is a district of the church under the pastoral care of a bishop. That includes the administration of certain functions concerned with the wider activity of the church as distinct from that at a local church level. Each diocese has a cathedral. In the Church of England there are 44 dioceses: 42 in England, one in the Diocese of Sodor and Man, and one in the Diocese of Europe of which 30 are in the Province of Canterbury and 14 in the Province of York. See www.cofe.anglican.org and also www.anglicansonline.org.

In the Church of Ireland there are seven dioceses in Northern Ireland and five in the Republic of Ireland.

See www.irelandanglican.org.

The Scottish Episcopal Church has seven dioceses: www.scotland.anglican.org. and the Church of Wales has six dioceses: www.churchinwales.org.uk.

The Roman Catholic Church has eight dioceses in Scotland, 22 in England and Wales and 26 in Ireland (six thought to be in Northern Ireland).

For a detailed explanation of a Roman Catholic diocese see the website www.newadvent.org.

Christ Church Cathedral is one of the oldest and most famous Christian structures in Britain and forms part of a World Heritage Site. It is the cathedral of the Archbishop of Canterbury, leader of the Church of England and symbolic leader of the worldwide Anglican Communion.

FIVE

ARCHITECT is the designer of the building who prepares the plans and arranges management of the construction, often a complex structure, and is occasionally known as 'creator': derived from Latin and Greek words meaning 'chief craftsman'. Occasionally there are effigies of such men, creators or masters, from earlier times as at Lincoln Cathedral with Richard of Gainsborough c.1300 who designed the fine 'Angel Choir'.

Few architects have the opportunity of designing a cathedral so in 1902 when the decision had been taken to build a great Anglican cathedral at Liverpool, there must have been a real sense of excitement. The name 'Scott' is one of the most famous names in the country in the field of church architecture including Sir George Gilbert Scott, especially at Chester, Lichfield and Edinburgh St. Mary's Episcopal. For the son, Giles Gilbert Scott, to be selected as a young architect to Liverpool Anglican Cathedral was a real challenge.

Liverpool was to be the largest church in Britain, and Scott said it fired his imagination.

The new cathedral at Coventry was built next to the old. Basil Spence had won the competition with his radical change from the Gothic original and was naturally criticised for his plan. When revealed in the press he received hundreds of letters and recalled that "80% were rude and the remaining 20% were very rude"! It is now an icon. Whilst medieval cathedrals took centuries, the new cathedral took as long to design, six years, as it did to build –1956-62.

Arundel RC Cathedral was begun by the 15th Duke of Norfolk in 1873 with an unusual architect, Joseph Hansom – inventor of the Hansom Cab – who created a great soaring church faced with Bath stone. In contrast, the modern Brentwood RC Cathedral from 1991 was designed by architect Quinlan Terry who took his inspiration from the early Italian Renaissance crossed with the English baroque of Christopher Wren, with the north elevation of nine bays each divided by Doric pilasters (an architectural element in classical architecture used to give the appearance of a supporting column), and broken by a huge, half-circular portico, which was inspired by a similar one at St. Paul's.

Part of the epitaph on the tomb of Sir Christopher Wren, architect of St. Paul's Cathedral, London is:

"Lector, si monumentum requiris, circumspice"
– *"Reader, if you seek a memorial, look around you"*.

St. Paul's was his great achievement, but we now know that many architects did not design all the buildings credited to them as they employed designers, master craftsmen and apprentices to play a significant part in the creation of a building.

A name of an architect, (builder, designer or engineer) is not normally given within this text, but there is an Appendix B about some of the more famous architects. One tends to forget the other key people in the building of a cathedral and certainly others such as the engineer are crucial especially for the structure. If one wishes to read a detailed, illuminating and fascinating story of the design, building and early management of a cathedral then that of Liverpool Anglican Cathedral is riveting: The Building of Liverpool Cathedral by Peter Kennerley, 1991: see Further Reading.

Architecture is therefore the art or science of building and a term only about 400 years old, for in medieval times a 'creator or master' would be a competent person acting on behalf of an abbot or bishop.There are mainly eight defined periods of architectural styles, with approximate dates:

Norman/Romanesque	1050 – 1150
Early English Gothic	1150 – 1250
Decorated Gothic	1250 – 1350
Perpendicular Gothic	1350 – 1550
Renaissance	17th century
Neo-Classical	18th century
Neo-Gothic	19th century
Modern	20th century and onwards.

Medieval styles are illustrated next in an excellent article, reproduced by courtesy of the editor and founder of 'Britain Express' David Ross (www.britainexpress.com), that describes the background to the architecture and art of cathedrals and churches.

Medieval Architecture

Art in the Middle Ages was inseparable from religion. It was infused with spiritual symbolism and meaning. The purpose of art was to awe and inspire the viewer with the grandeur of God. It also served to symbolise what people believed. Pope Gregory the Great, he of the Gregorian chants, said, "painting can do for the illiterate what writing does for those who read." He might have added that sculpture could serve the same purpose.

Church Sculpture. The mission of the sculptor, whose work was seen almost exclusively adorning church buildings, was to educate as well as decorate. He brought Biblical tales and moral lessons to life in stone. Carvings were not just religious, however. Everywhere you look there is evidence of pre-Christian symbology in church sculpture; animals real and fanciful, scenes of everyday life, and the pagan 'Green Man' peering out from amongst carefully wrought leaves and vines of stone. Sculpture burst forth gloriously in the Romanesque era, with little regard for classical conventions of proportion of figures.

Chapel of St. John at the Tower of London – a good example of early Romanesque style

The Romanesque Period. At the beginning of the Norman era the style of architecture that was in vogue was known as Romanesque, because it copied the pattern and proportion of the architecture of the Roman Empire. The chief characteristics of the Romanesque style were barrel vaults, round arches, thick piers, and few windows.

The easiest point to look for is the rounded arch, seen in door openings and windows. In general the Romanesque churches were heavy and solid, carrying about them an air of solemnity and gloom. These early Norman churches were not always so stark as they seem today, however. In their heyday the church walls were hung with tapestries or painted richly. The statues of the saints were gilded (on some you can still see traces of the paint if you look closely), and the service books were inlaid with gold, jewels, and ivory. Chalices and reliquaries were encrusted with gems.

The Gothic Style. Beginning in 12th century France a new style of architecture and decoration emerged. At the time it was called simply 'The French Style', but later Renaissance critics, appalled at the abandonment of classical line and proportion, derisively called it 'Gothic'. This was a reference to the imagined lack of culture of the barbarian tribes, including the Goths, which had ransacked Rome in the twilight of the Roman Empire.

Gothic architecture is light, spacious, and graceful. Advances in architectural technique learned from contacts with the Arab world during the Crusades led to innovations such as the pointed arch, ribbed vault, and the buttress. Heavy Romanesque piers were replaced by slender clusters of columns. Window sizes grew enormously, as did the height of vaults and spires. Sculpture became free standing rather than being incorporated in columns.

A late Gothic chantry chapel at Winchester cathedral

The new expanse of window space was filled with gloriously rich coloured glass. The easiest point of reference to look for in a Gothic church is the pointed arch, seen in window openings and doors. Also, the later Gothic churches had very elaborate decoration, especially the 'tracery', or stonework supporting the stained glass windows.

Church Building. Churches were a point of civic pride, and towns vied to outdo each other in the glory of their churches. Money for the church was raised by the sale of indulgences, fund raising caravans of relics, parish contributions, and donations from nobles. Many times a guild would pay for a stained glass window depicting their trade. Often people would volunteer their labour to the construction, though much of the work was carried on by skilled workmen under the watchful eye of the head mason and the architect.

Church Siting and Orientation. Churches were often sited on pre-Christian sites of spiritual importance, taking advantage of people's existing devotion to a particular place. Worship was carried on in the same place, just with a Christian orientation. Speaking of orientation, churches are nearly always oriented so that the main altar is at the east end of the church, facing Jerusalem and, not coincidentally, the rising sun. Even if the altar end of the church is not literally in the east, that end is still referred to as the east end. In theory, then, the east end of an English church could face west.

Gothic Architecture in England

Gothic architecture in Britain has been neatly divided into four periods, or styles. The person who did the dividing that has been obediently followed by subsequent generations of writers and historians was Thomas Rickman (1776-1841). In his 1817 work *"An Attempt to Discriminate the Styles of English Architecture from the Conquest to the Reformation"* (whew! what a mouthful!) Rickman labelled the styles *Norman, Early English, Decorated*, and *Perpendicular*.

King's College Chapel, Cambridge

Like any classification system in the arts these styles cannot be dogmatically assigned dates, but for the sake of simplicity let's do it anyway.

The term 'Gothic' itself needs some explaining. The original style of building – one might call it a philosophy of architecture – sprang up in the Ile de France, and was known during the Middle Ages as 'the French Style'. It was not until the 16th century that art critic Giorgio Vassari derisively compared medieval architecture to the barbarism (and presumed lack of taste) of the Goths who had ravaged Rome. It was only then that the term 'Gothic' came into vogue.

So what were the characteristics of a Gothic building? Generally speaking, Gothic architecture emphasised strong vertical lines, high vaulted ceilings, minimal wall space, pointed window and door openings, and buttressed walls. But these characteristic Gothic themes did not spring into being overnight. Let's see how the style of Gothic architecture evolved in Britain.

The Norman Gothic period (1066-1200) wasn't a whole lot different from Gothic elsewhere in Europe. The British temperament had yet to stamp its own mark on the new "French style". The buildings of this time are

Wells Cathedral

transitional – many still have the thick piers and rounded window openings of the earlier Romanesque style. Vaulting and decoration are simple; there is little sign of the elaborate stonework to come. Some good examples of the Norman Gothic period are: Durham Cathedral, Wells Cathedral, and Ely Cathedral (west tower 1150-75).

It is in the Early English period (1200-1275) that the Gothic style became truly adapted by English craftsmen/ architects. This period is also called "Lancet", referring to the pointed lancet windows (narrow, untraceried) that characterise it. Form is still austere and proportion is magnificently simple.

The main points of Early English are: quadripartite ribbing in vaults, slender towers topped with spires, lancet windows – both single and grouped – and piers with narrow, clustered shafts. The finest example of Early English is to be found at Salisbury Cathedral.

Early English Gothic Architecture

The Early English period (1180-1275) marks the first flowering of English Gothic. The Gothic style evolved in France; indeed it was first called "The French Style", beginning in the middle of the 12th century.

If one can generalise about a style which spanned almost a century, we can characterise Early English by saying that it emphasised simple, almost austere lines, preferring fine proportion to elaborate decoration. Early English emphasises height, as if the builders were reaching for the sky. In a sense, they were, as church building was a symbolic expression of religious aspiration. Church architecture in particular had to symbolise Christian thought to a largely illiterate population. Thus even decorative touches such as carvings and statues of saints had to tell a story to people who could not read.

The major distinction between the Early English and the Norman, or Romanesque period, which preceded it, is the use of the pointed arch. The pointed arch allowed a whole range of new building expression

Early English church elevations. Note the flying buttresses on the right

to take place; arches could span greater distances, allowing vaults to be taller and wider. The arch could support greater weight, allowing walls to be thinner and pierced by wider window openings. This in turn encouraged the use of stained glass. The simple buttresses of the Norman period gave way to flying buttresses, which distributed the weight and thrust of roofs and walls right down to the ground. These flying buttresses may be visible over the aisles, but just as often were concealed in the aisle roof. Another variation on the Early English

"Oxford" buttress

buttress is the "Oxford buttress", set diagonally at corners.

Towers were topped with steeply pitched roofs, often surmounted with very slender towers emerging from a broach, or pyramidal base.

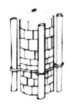

Early English pier

The massive columns of the Romanesque period were replaced with thin clusters of shafts, often built of dark Purbeck marble. The capitals of shafts were often richly carved, with highly stylised foliage designs being popular. The richness of these carvings was due in part to the introduction of the chisel in stone carving. Previously, carving had been done with axes, necessitating low relief and fairly simple designs.

The introduction of the chisel allowed a great deal more artistic control and we see undercutting become extremely popular. Carvings stand out from the underlying stone and are much more three-dimensional than in the Norman Romanesque period.

Early in the 13th century windows were primarily of a simple, untraceried (lancet) design, either single or grouped together. Later designs favoured two or three lights grouped under a single dripstone.

Early English foliage carving

Where the hood moulding (dripstone) followed a pointed design, echoing the lines of the windows,

Window

the architects put small ornamental holes in the space between the moulding and the lancets. This approach is called Plate Tracery. As plate tracery developed, the small holes became more elaborate, evolving into ornate trefoil and quatrefoil designs.

Major Early English buildings to visit in England:

The most complete example of Early English is without a doubt to be seen at Salisbury Cathedral. Salisbury is unique in that it was built within a short time span (c1200-1275), thus its architectural style, with the exception of the 14th century tower and spire, is fairly uncluttered by later additions and alterations.

Other Early English buildings to visit include Wells Cathedral (interior), St. Bartholomew's (London), Lincoln Cathedral, and Westminster Abbey nave (1245-1270)

The Decorated Gothic Period

The Decorated Period (1280-1380) is the second phase of Gothic architecture in England. Other common names used to refer to this period are Middle Pointed, Curvilinear, Geometric, and Flamboyant. All these terms refer to the shape of window heads

Decorated window evolution

and window tracery, which became much more elaborate and, well, "decorated"! The shape of buildings did not change radically, rather the Decorated period was one of evolution, rather than revolution. Widespread adoption of the flying buttress to distribute the load of walls and roof made possible the use of wider, taller windows, and with the increase in size came a corresponding

Decorated period vaulting

increase in decorative elements in the window head. More complex patterns of stone vaulting also meant that walls needed to carry less of the building's weight and thrust, therefore window openings in walls were free to fulfil more decorative functions.

The simple geometric shapes of the Early English period gave way to complex curves; the ogee arch being the most obvious. The ogee combines a convex and a concave curve in the same arch. This double-curve is the basis of most of the curvilinear tracery which became so popular during the 14th century.

The vaulting of the Early English period became lighter, and short ribs sprouted from the main ribs to form star-shaped patterns that were as much ornamental as structural. The place where the ribs met became a focal point for decorative touches such as pendant knobs, grotesque faces, or foliage.

Decorated style foliage carving

As with the preceding Early English period, carving in the Decorated period is focussed on foliage patterns, though the Decorated designs are more curvaceous than the Early English. A wider variety of leaves are used; with ivy, oak, rose, and vines leading the way. Animals, birds, and human figures are interspersed with foliage, and all the forms are more natural, less stiffly formal than Early English.

Other common ornamental carving features are the ball-flower (a partly opened flower set on a sphere within a hollow moulding) and the symmetrical four-leaved flower. Tombs and monuments within a church are frequently covered in foliage carvings. The evolution of the column continued, though no startling change of form occurs. Rather, the columns became more slender, and the free-standing shafts of the Early English period gave way to clusters of columns making up larger piers.

Although stone was still the most popular building medium, certainly for churches and the houses of the well-to-do, brick made some inroads for the first time since the departure of the Romans. These bricks were introduced from the Netherlands, where they were quite popular, and made the strongest impression in East Anglia, due to simple geographic proximity to the source. Bricks were used almost entirely for secular buildings, and even then their use was not widespread.

Major examples of Decorated style in England: Lichfield Cathedral, Exeter Cathedral.

Perpendicular Gothic Architecture

The style we know as Perpendicular Gothic is the final phase of Gothic architecture in England, after the Early English and Decorated periods, and it lasted by far the longest of the three periods, stretching from the late 14th until the early 16th century. As its name suggests, the chief characteristic of Perpendicular architecture is the emphasis on strong vertical lines, seen most markedly in window tracery and wall panelling. Roof vaulting became elaborate and

Perpendicular cathedral

ornate, with a multitude of vaulting ribs spreading outwards in a fan shape, ornamented with pendants and cross-ribs that served a purely decorative function. Perhaps the finest examples of Perpendicular fan vaulting survive at King's College Chapel, Cambridge (1446-1515), and Henry VII's Chapel at Westminster Cathedral (1503-1519).

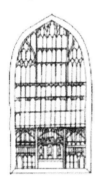

Perpendicular window

The flying buttress reached its final graceful and highly decorated form, with knobs, crockets and small pinnacles adorning every possible surface. Windows were the "artist's palette" of the Perpendicular builders; because of advances in the use of the pointed arch and supporting elements such as the flying buttress, window openings could be extremely large, and builders took advantage of their opportunity to create huge expanses of glass separated by thin, curving stone tracery in ever more elaborate patterns. Window area was maximised, while wall area was minimised. The result is lofty, open interiors of extraordinary lightness and delicacy.

Another notable characteristic of Perpendicular Gothic are the superb hammerbeam roofs, where advances in joinery and a better understanding of how to distribute the load and thrust of ceiling weight allowed roofs which spanned great open spaces. The hammerbeam roof is the wooden equivalent of the stone vaulting used in the

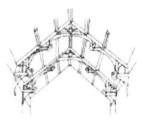

Hammerbeam roof

great cathedrals of the time. Simply put, hammerbeam construction makes use of short horizontal and vertical beams to distribute the weight of a roof. These short beams rise in steps from the top of a wall to the roof peak, creating a more open space than earlier techniques allowed.

Although the timbers which made up the supporting elements in hammerbeam roofs were structural, they were also used as ornamental elements. The meeting places of timbers were often adorned with pendants or fanciful carvings, and the timbers themselves were often painted and gilded. The best examples of hammerbeam roofs are to be found in East Anglia, particularly the churches of Norfolk.

Hood moulding over doors was squared off, rather than echoing the pointed arch opening of the door itself. Piers were still constructed of clusters of thin shafts, as in the Decorated period, but the separation between the shafts was not so pronounced; the separate shafts

Perpendicular pier cross-section

becoming more like simple folds of stone on the surface of the pier.

Perpendicular foliage design

The curvilinear carving which so characterised the Decorated period became more formal, less flowing. Foliage designs were still the most popular motif, but even these are more stiff and formal, less ebullient, and certainly less natural. Carvings are shallower, and stand out very little from the surface of their stone background.

Major Perpendicular Gothic buildings to visit:
Westminster Hall, London. King's College Chapel, Cambridge
Henry VII's Chapel at Westminster Cathedral, London
Bath Abbey
Winchester Cathedral nave.
(End of article)

The most definitive example of Romanesque style in England may be seen at Durham Cathedral, where the Norman work is largely unaltered by later additions. Here also one can see the first attempts at ribbed vaulting which would later evolve into the full-blown Gothic style in the 13th century. It is said that here the three main innovations of the revolutionary Gothic style come together: pointed arches, ribbed vaults and flying buttresses.

(Durham and York are architecturally and historically two of the most important cathedrals: York was built in the Gothic style of almost every stage of Gothic architecture but it was once a Norman cathedral and commenced before Durham – the only remains of the Norman part are in the minster crypt. One of the key differences between Durham Cathedral and York Minster is that Durham had a monastery attached to it. The buildings of the monastery – dissolved in 1540 – were around the cloister on the south side of the cathedral.)

Gothic style has been described as an encyclopaedia as it tries to display everything!

Liverpool Anglican Cathedral, built from 1904 to around 1968, is often described as 'Gothic' or 'Neo-Gothic' but it really should not be put into any category, for as John

Betjeman said: "it is the art of enclosing space" and does not really represent one fashion.

Major Romanesque cathedrals to visit in England are: Durham, Ely, Gloucester, Rochester, Southwell and of course Canterbury, where a major Anglo-Saxon cathedral has been recently revealed under the flagstones of the current nave. Another surviving example of Romanesque architecture is the White Tower at the Tower of London, where the Chapel of St. John in the Tower displays superbly the rounded Romanesque arch.

Hereford is one of the smaller cathedrals of England, and is an architectural gem for, in the opinion of Sir Gilbert Scott, few English cathedrals have a more perfect series of specimens of the different styles of English architecture. The visitor can see here examples of all the fashions of architecture in use in this country during the five centuries preceding the 16th.

Bath Abbey is the last of the great medieval churches of England, begun in 1499 with a unique west front depicting the dream of its founder. Beverley Minster is confirmed as one of the most beautiful Gothic churches in Europe with three styles of Early English, Decorated and Perpendicular architecture. Notable also are Carlisle, Chester, Lichfield and Worcester – all built of red sandstone that wears and needs more restoration. St. Machar's in Old Aberdeen is the only granite medieval cathedral in the world, located on the edge of a small hill above a park (Machar was a disciple of St. Columba and was told by God in a dream to leave Iona, go east and found a church by a river shaped like a bishop's crook, just the shape of the River Don at this point).

We should remember that architecture and building were at the 'cutting edge' of technology, and errors of judgement could lead to the collapse of buildings: for example the central towers at Lincoln and Winchester.

Salisbury however, built from 70,000 tons of stone with 3,000 tons of timber for the roof covered with 450 tons of lead, and with foundations reported to be only four feet deep, escaped disaster even when the imposing large spire was added, although the columns of the central crossing are 'bowed' by some inches.

Lincoln is an impressive tribute to British medieval architecture:

surviving through a series of disasters from the 12th century when fire destroyed its roof, only to be rebuilt and destroyed again and again by earthquake, gales and fire that savaged the building until the 16th century; perhaps now protected by the 'Lincoln Imp', peering down on visitors and ready to pounce! An excellent website to view the 'animated history' of development of a cathedral – Lincoln Cathedral – is a memorial site to artist Peter Fairweather, deceased: www.churchmousewebsite.co.uk.

SIX

ARCHITRAVE is a main beam resting immediately on the abacus (the upper member) of a column; various parts surrounding a doorway or window, or a moulding round the exterior of an arch. Also:

ARCHIVOLT is an ornamental moulding (or 'molding') that follows the curve of the underside of an arch, and is composed of bands of ornamental mouldings surrounding an arched opening, corresponding to the architrave in the case of a rectangular opening. The word is sometimes used to refer to the under-side or inner curve of the arch itself (known as the intrados) and originates in the Italian (or French) equivalents of the English words arch and vault. See also tympanum.

ARCHIVE is a place in which collected records are stored, sometimes linked to a chapter house or library. The 900th anniversary of the death of Anselm, saint, theologian, Archbishop of Canterbury, and one of the medieval builders of Canterbury Cathedral occurred in 2009: the Canterbury archive holds some significant printed editions of Anselm's works and a number of interesting documents from his time as Archbishop. The archive at Durham is of 11th-20th century muniments (documents kept as evidence) exceptionally well-preserved since 1539. The bulk of the archives of St. Paul's London was transferred to the manuscripts section of the Guildhall Library in September 1980 for safekeeping.

There is a Cathedral Libraries and Archives Association – see website: cofe.anglican.org

ARTEFACT: a product of human art and workmanship – a sculpture, the Green Man, window banner and possibly the most important, silver and the stained glass – often as a memorial. A satisfying challenge is to find the oldest artefact in each cathedral or a Christian-based artefact in a museum, and sense history.

Whilst cathedrals have many beautiful historic artefacts there are also outstanding specimens in fine museums, notably the Victoria and Albert Museum in London that has, for example, a beautiful reliquary casket of St. Thomas Becket, French-made about 10 years after Becket's murder in Canterbury Cathedral in 1170;

an exquisite 'St. Nicholas' Crozier, one of the finest surviving examples of medieval carving from 1160 in ivory of an abbot or bishop's staff – with the story of the 'Annunciation of the Shepherds' and the 'birth of St. Nicholas';

a unique walrus ivory made in England (1190-1200) that depicts Judas at the Last Supper, perhaps part of an altar: a very strong image showing Judas cowering on the floor, almost dog-like, being fed from the hand of Christ;

the Gloucester Candlestick, English from 1104 – 1113, a rare example of English Romanesque metalwork full of plants and figures from dogs to dragons, formerly a treasure of Le Mans Cathedral until the 18th century, and then a gift to the Abbey Church of St. Peter, now Gloucester Cathedral. The Apostles Matthew, Mark, Luke and John are represented by an angel, a lion, an ox and an eagle. A main inscription in Latin is: *"The burden of light is the work of virtue. Shining doctrine teaches that man be not shadowed by vice."*

Possibly the most unusual is an English golden reliquary cross from 900-1000, said from recent conservation examination to contain 'a human finger and a human head louse'! Made of cedar wood, covered with sheets of gold, the front is decorated with filigree work, enamels and a walrus ivory figure of Christ held in place by golden nails through his palms.

At Bristol Anglican Cathedral in the south transept there is a Saxon stone, one of the finest from before the Norman Conquest, named 'The Harrowing of Hell'.

In Scotland, there is the remarkable story of the artefact, 'the Stone of Destiny', when King Edward I of England seized the stone and took it to Westminster where it remained under the Confessor's Coronation Chair for 700 years until 'reclaimed' by Scottish adventurers and returned to Scotland. It is now housed in Edinburgh Castle: there is still the unanswered question – is it the real Stone of Destiny?

This decorative and modern panel around a column in Hereford Cathedral is part of a story in the history of the cathedral. (Shown on page 58)

In 1988 John Hull created the project 'Cathedrals through Touch and Hearing' to enable blind visitors especially to appreciate the architecture: artefacts, carved wooden models and elevated ground plans have been placed in 17 English cathedrals at Birmingham, Canterbury, Chichester, Coventry,

Durham, Exeter, Gloucester, Hereford, Lichfield, Lincoln, Norwich, Peterborough, Saint Albans, Salisbury, Winchester, Worcester, and York Minster.

AUMBREY, or aumbry or almery, formerly a cupboard for alms, is the cupboard or reserved space in the chancel, sometimes in the reredos or near the sedilia, and rarely seen, that is used for the storage of sacred vessels. In Anglican churches and cathedrals the aumbry often houses the blessed sacrament of consecrated bread and wine reserved for the Communion of the sick and housebound and as a focus of personal devotion.

SEVEN

BALL-FLOWER (or ballflower) is an ornament in stone-masonry in the form of a ball inserted in the cup of a flower. The decorative feature is said to have come to Britain with the Normans, flowering in the 13-14th century, with the earliest known in the west part of Salisbury Cathedral. It seems then  to have been used more frequently, where at Gloucester Cathedral in the south side, it is in profusion – as seen in the photograph.

Ball-flowers are unusual, as it is said that no two are identical, carved largely freehand, often crudely. They are generally placed in rows at equal distances in the hollow of a moulding, frequently by the sides of mullions. Though based on a standard pattern of three petals surrounding a central ball or sphere, some rogue four-petalled examples occur.

Hereford Cathedral is famous for its central tower decorated with thousands of carved stone ball-flowers, having probably the largest number of them to be found anywhere on one building. (Its tower opened again to visitors in 2007 following a three-year £600,000 restoration when repairs had been carried out to the leaded roof and three pinnacles at the top of the tower, as well as several hundred ball-flower sculptures).

BAPTISTRY (or Baptistery, a term not often used nowadays) is a bay or corner or even a chapel of a cathedral reserved for baptisms, and provided with a font, usually near the west door: sometimes a screen or grille 'screens' the baptistry from the nave.

The 81 ft. high 'Baptistery' window at Coventry, shown here, is glorious and breathtaking, containing a total of 195 lights of stained glass in bright primary colours designed by John Piper, with the Stone of Bethlehem for a font just in front.

The baptistry at Chester, created in 1855 with a font from Venice in the same year, has part of the original Norman Abbey of 1140, found at the lower stages of what was to be a Tower.

BATIK is a method of printing coloured designs on textiles, that originated in Java, by waxing parts not to be dyed. Winchester Cathedral is noted for its 16 Batiks, made in 1979 by the late Thetis Blacker of the 'creation and redemption', hanging as banners during festivals.

BEAK-HEAD: a Romanesque carving in the form of a series of animal, bird (think of the heron), or humanoid heads with long pointed beaks (or tongues) curving around a lower roll-moulding, as in a church doorway. (Heads with stumpier cone-like beaks are cats' heads).

The beak-head found decorating the arches of Norman and Romanesque churches is one of the most intriguing forms of sculpture: nightmarish heads of birds, beasts or monsters stare down from the arch as if to frighten the visitor. Human heads occasionally appear, with their tongues or beards lying across the angle roll of the arch, as at Lincoln Cathedral.

(Beak-head is also the description of the protruding part of the foremost section of a sailing ship, fitted on sailing vessels from the 16th to the 18th century that served as a working platform by sailors working the sails of the bowsprit, the forward-pointing mast that carries the spritsails, and one of the most ornate sections of a ship, particularly in the extravagant Baroque-style ships of the 17th century, often decorated with carved statues).

BELFRY is the bell tower or 'campanile': usually applied only to a bell tower that is detached from the church – one example still survives at Chichester c.1410.

(By the mid-1200s a spire was built on top of the bell tower which had been located at the centre of the cathedral and this made the bell tower unstable. By the early 1400s a separate bell tower was built and can still be seen today off the west end of the cathedral – this building is probably the basis of the present cathedral. There are eight bells in the bell tower and a team of 15 bell-ringers climb the 84 steps every Sunday and Wednesday).

BELLS: a name with many meanings, (for example even relating to a flower such as Canterbury Bell and of course bluebell: as a bell-shaped object), but is primarily a hollow object of cast metal in a deep cup shape, widening at the lip and made to emit clear musical sound when struck.

Bell metal is the alloy of copper and tin (more tin than in bronze) for bells, usually made in a foundry. A major foundry for cathedral bells is that at Whitechapel Foundry in London (that is open by special arrangement to visitors).

Historic bells are found at Liverpool's Anglican Cathedral that can be heard for miles around:

At 220ft (67m) above floor level, the bells are the highest and heaviest ringing peal in the world with 13 bells, named the Bartlett Bells after Thomas Bartlett, a Liverpool man who bequeathed the funding. They weigh a total of 16.5 tons and are grouped in a circle around the great 14.5 ton bourdon bell, named 'Great George'. The bells vary in size and note, from the light 9cwt treble to the tenor at 4.1tons. The 13th bell (sharp 2nd) is extra to the main peal, to make possible ringing in a correct octave in a higher key. All 13 bells were cast at Whitechapel Foundry, London. The 'Great George' bourdon bell was cast by Taylors of Loughborough and at 14.5 tons is the second most massive bell in Britain: named in memory of King George V, this bell is hung in a pendant position and sounded by means of a counter-balanced clapper. A vivid description of the awesome task in building and tuning, and in creating the necessary support structure in the tower is in 'The Building of Liverpool Cathedral'. (See Further Reading.)

Only the 16.5 ton 'Great Paul' of St. Pauls, London is heavier.

The second heaviest bells in the world are said to be at All Saints Church in Inverary, Scotland. Other reports state that the heaviest ringing peals in England are at Exeter and St. Paul's London, so perhaps there are different definitions of the heaviest bells.

St. Paul's, definitely, has the second largest ring of bells in the world that are hung for change ringing: there are 12 bells in the North West Tower dating from 1878. While there are a number of churches and cathedrals that have 12 bells, they are not that common and it is rare to have bells of such a size, donated by the Corporation and a number of the City livery companies. In addition to the 12 bells there is the original service bell affectionately known as 'The Banger', cast by Philip Wightman in 1700 when the building of the West Tower was completed. It remained alone for 178 years until the ring of 12 bells was cast in 1878 and is still rung prior to the 08:00 Eucharist.

Norwich is one of only three Anglican cathedrals which does not have a set of bells hung for full-circle change ringing (the other two are Ely and Salisbury). The Norman central tower at Norwich contains five bells, which are hung 'dead' and chimed by the clock and as service bells.

St. Magnus in Orkney is unique among British cathedrals for its use of a Norwegian style of bell-ringing known as 'clocking', where just one bell-ringer can operate the bells by hand and using foot-pedals (proof of the strong Viking influence on the island). For enthusiasts, much more detail is at this website: www.1911encyclopedia.org/Bell

EIGHT

BIBLE: the Holy Book contains the Christian scriptures of the Old and New Testaments. The King James Version of the Bible remains the most widely published text in the English language. Many English translations of the Bible have appeared in the centuries since the King James, but no other has had such an impact, described as *"the noblest monument of English prose"*.

It was the work of around 50 scholars who were appointed in 1604 by King James 1, and it is dedicated to him. James VI & I (1567 – 1625) was King of Scots as James VI from 1567 to 1625, and King of England and Ireland as James 1 from 1603 to 1625 and during this period the 'golden age' of literature prospered. It was in the winter of 1610 in the Stationers' Hall next to St. Paul's London that the translators gathered together to read the product of their work and to approve the final version, so that 400 years of potent poetry were celebrated in 2011. (See the Trust's website: www.kingjamesbibletrust.org)

A new book by Melvyn Bragg: *'The Book of Books: The radical impact of the King James Bible 1611-2022'* reveals the extraordinary and still-felt impact of a work created 400 years ago. Lord Bragg states: *"You may be a Christian. You may be anti-Christian, or of another religion or none. You may be an atheist fundamentalist and think the Bible is monstrous, a book to be dismissed or derided. But whoever you are in the English-speaking world, I hope to persuade you to consider that the King James Bible has driven the making of that world over the last 400 years, often in the most unanticipated ways."* (See Further Reading.)

An 1853 edition, printed in Oxford, was used by Abraham Lincoln when he swore the oath of office at his inauguration in 1861 as President of the United States of America, and similarly used by Barack Obama at his inauguration in Washington DC in January 2009.

St. Asaph in Wales is noted for the fact that the first translation of the Bible into Welsh was by its bishop, William Morgan, 1604, who is buried there.

Winchester is home to the 'Winchester Bible', the best example of a 12th century Bible in the country.

Lichfield has a hand-produced English language 'Wycliffe Bible', created at a time when even possessing a copy of the Bible in English was a capital offence: only 20 such Bibles are thought to exist today. In addition, the cathedral owns a first edition 1539 Great Bible (the first authorised English language Bible ever printed), a first edition copy of this first issue 1611 Bible, and a first edition of the second issue 1611 Bible, known as the 'Judas Bible' because of a misprint where the name 'Jesus' in Matthew 26: 36 appears as 'Judas': all to be displayed at the cathedral.

BOOK of HOURS was a devotional book popular in the Middle Ages. It is the most common type of surviving medieval illuminated manuscript. It has its origin in the

Psalter, which monks and nuns were required to recite, and by the 12th century this had developed into the Breviary, with weekly cycles of readings which changed with the liturgical season. Most contained the Office of the Blessed Virgin Mary, the prayers, psalms and readings for private devotional use. Eventually a selection of texts was produced in much shorter volumes and came to be called a book of hours, often purchased and used by lay-people. Books were embellished according to the taste and pocket of the person for whom they were prepared and widely used by the devout laity, from the 13th century onwards. Many Books of Hours were made for women with some evidence that they were given as a wedding present from a husband to his bride. The earliest surviving English example was apparently written for a laywoman living in or near Oxford in about 1240. It is smaller than a modern paperback but heavily illuminated with major initials, but no full-page miniatures. In the 14th century the Book of Hours overtook the Psalter as the most common example of lavish illumination. By the 15th century, there are also examples of servants owning their own Books of Hours. Frequently they were passed down through the family as recorded in wills. It is reported that after defeating Richard III, Henry VII gave Richard's Book of Hours to his mother, who modified it to include her name. Heraldry was usually erased or over-painted by new owners. The Books form an important record of life in the 15th and 16th centuries as well as the study of medieval Christianity.

(One famous book is Cardinal Stuart's Book of Hours dating from around 1500 and follows the usual pattern of beginning each Hour with a miniature depicting an episode in the Virgin Mary's life. The miniature for Sext – the sixth hour of the day – shows the Adoration of the Three Kings. This special Book of Hours was rebound for Henry Benedict, Cardinal Stuart, in red velvet with gilt clasps, embroidered with silk, gold and sequins. In the centre of each board are the Stuart Royal Arms, surmounted by a royal crown, along with a cardinal's hat and tassels. The binding was almost certainly created after the death of his elder brother, Prince Charles Edward Stuart -Bonnie Prince Charlie- in 1788. The copy is believed to be in the Royal Collection).

NINE

BOSS: (See also roof bosses). In medieval architecture a Boss was a keystone carved ornamentally and occasionally painted and gilded at the intersection of ribs in a vaulted roof.

It is a necessity as the meeting place of the ribs, and craftsmen first used the opportunity for special enrichment. Norwich has a thousand roof bosses, more than any other cathedral, that run the whole length of the nave; an amazing collection of late medieval sculpture covering a huge variety of subjects where most of them tell a story. This is one of the greatest collections of bible stories in stone, from creation to doomsday: alongside the lives of saints there are mysterious Green Men peeping out of green foliage, and fearsome grotesque

The best known boss in the nave of Exeter Cathedral, shown here, is the assassination of Thomas Becket in 1170. Whilst the Boss was undoubtedly painted in 1300 it is unlikely that it was as shown in this modern redecoration.

strange creatures, half beast, half human lurking with intent.

There are over 400 carved bosses in Exeter Cathedral; the large central ones weighing over two tons – imagine the feat of lifting these over 60 feet high using only primitive mechanical means. These show mythical creatures such as mermaids and dragons, and many living creatures and other stories.

In the south transept at York the bosses were largely destroyed during the 1984 fire, but modern replacements include six designed by children in a television competition.

BRASSES are inscribed monuments or memorials – a tablet often engraved with the figures of a person or persons buried in the grave beneath, or placed on an adjacent wall. Brass is a yellow alloy of copper and zinc. Approximately 8,000 brasses have survived – a small fraction of what once existed, and mainly in the southern and eastern counties of England where wool and trade with the continent created the considerable wealth required to have a brass made between the 13th and 15th centuries. Often now in a cathedral, there are almost complete pavements of empty indented slabs where brasses would have once been. Lincoln, for example, has over 200 empty slabs – not one brass survives. Although monumental brasses vary in age, quality and historic interest, the best and most ancient of them are very important medieval antiquities. They deserve our respect and sensitivity, especially when they are to be touched, handled or moved.

Brass rubbing is a special hobby often encouraged for children, and adults, in historic buildings, but only with permission to ensure protection of the tablet. Ask a guide in a cathedral for the location of important and historic brass dating mainly from the 13ᵗʰ to 17ᵗʰ centuries. There are some notable old brasses also at Carlisle, Ely, Chichester, Exeter, Oxford, St. Albans and Salisbury Cathedrals, and in York Minster.

The south transept of Hereford displays a number of very good medieval brasses similar to that here.

Linked with a trail, Manchester has workshops on brass rubbing.

BUTTRESS is a vertical mass of brickwork or masonry to stiffen the wall, and one that projects from a wall to resist the outward thrust of a roof-truss or vault. Note 'Flying Buttress' that is an arch to serve as a prop, with the upper end resting against the high main wall, its lower end against a pier.

Those at Bath Abbey are notable.

The building of the new cathedral at Chichester, in the centre of the Roman former town, began around 1076 and continued into the twelfth century, but fires in 1114 and 1187 completely destroyed the timber roof and caused extensive damage to the arcade stonework. Restoration then included the introduction of stone vaulting and the addition of Purbeck marble shafts at ground and clerestory level: externally, flying buttresses were added.

TEN

CANON comes from the Latin 'Canonicus', originally from the Greek word 'kanonicos' – meaning 1) rule, measuring stick or standard; 2) formulation, schedule or assignment; and 3) 'rule of faith' as used in the 2nd century church, leading to 'canon' of truth. It is a complicated history linked with the Bible and subject to much research especially comparing the teachings with the 'measuring stick (i.e., canon) of truth'.

A CANON now is a priest or minister who is a member of certain bodies of the Christian clergy subject to an ecclesiastical rule (canon).

Originally a canon was a cleric living with others in a clergy-house, and later in one of the houses within the precinct or close of a cathedral and ordering his life according to the orders or rules of the church. This way of life is first documented in the 8th century. In the 11th century, some churches required clergy thus living together to adopt the first rule proposed by St. Augustine that they renounce private wealth. Those who embraced this change were known as Augustinians or Canons Regular, whilst those who did not were known as secular canons. Since the Reformation all canons of the Church of England have been secular, although an individual canon may also be a member of a religious order. Mostly, however, they are ordained priests or members of the clergy usually in connection with a cathedral. A canon is a member of the chapter of priests, headed by the dean, which is responsible for administering a cathedral or certain other churches that are styled collegiate churches. The title of canon may still be given in many dioceses to senior parish priests as a largely honorary title and is usually given in recognition of long and dedicated service to the diocese. Honorary canons are members of the chapter in name but are non-residential and receive no emoluments. They are entitled to call themselves canon and have a role in the administration of the cathedral. Similarly in the Catholic Church, the members of the chapter of a cathedral or of a collegiate church (so called after their chapter) are Canons.

CANOPY, or Baldachin, had its beginnings as a cloth canopy, especially as a canopy of state over an altar or throne; a covering suspended normally over the High Altar, but it may be a sturdy, permanent architectural feature, particularly over high altars in cathedrals, where such a structure may be called a ciborium when it is sufficiently architectural in form.

That at Derby with its Corinthian columns, Roman Doric pillars and golden ceiling forms part of Sebastian Comper's design for the eastern extension of the cathedral. At Winchester the choir stalls have magnificent gabled canopies, elaborately carved with flowers and plants, owls and monkeys, dragons, knights and Green Men.

At Beverley Minster is a stone-carved percy canopy, one of the masterpieces of English decorated stone, 1340-1349.

At St. Albans a 20th century addition is an embroidered canopy for the shrine of St. Alban.

CAPITAL is a head or cornice of a pillar or column; the top of a column that supports the arches, often carved with foliage or as a scene illustrating a moral story or a biblical scene. Although richly ornamental it serves a useful purpose to distribute weight from above on to the shaft of the column.

12th-century Romanesque carved capitals in St. Anselm's Chapel, Canterbury Cathedral.

Carlisle has capitals that depict months of the year.

Southwell, near Nottingham, has chapter house capitals with special foliage. Wells has apple pickers (or 'scrumpers') in a foliate style known as 'stiff leaf', and York Minster has very early English styles.

Unusual are those at Belfast Cathedral: 22 columns and capitals outside the porches, columns alternately carved and plain, and, as in every other part of the cathedral, no two capitals are alike in design.

Belfast Cathedral – Entrance and Capitals

CARPET of FLOWERS is a special celebration of Corpus Christi Day, 60 days after Easter, and especially at Arundel RC Cathedral where the whole aisle is a vast bed of flowers laid by the congregation, a tradition here since 1877.

(Apparently, Duke Henry, having seen the carpet of flowers in the village of Sutri outside Rome, introduced the practice to Arundel in 1877. The tradition was broken during the First World War but revived in 1919, and has continued ever since, with parishioners undertaking the elaborate preparations).

CARRELS are small study spaces or enclosures in a cloister or library; cubicles usually where the monks studied and wrote their manuscripts, as seen in Chester and Gloucester Cathedrals.

CASSOCK is a long close garment, usually black, worn by the clergy and choristers.

(See also robes).

CATHEDRA: the name cathedral originates from the Greek word (*kathedra*) representing the bishop's seat or throne, often ornate and splendidly carved in wood, with the tradition that he would sit here and teach his clergy. The bishop's seat is usually at the east end of the quire near to the Sanctuary and its high altar, the focal point of a cathedral.

The cathedra in Durham Cathedral is said to be the highest anywhere. That at Derby is Greek Orthodox in origin, the upper part of a 16th century icon stand and the 17th century seat from Constantinople with outstanding decorative features. Possibly the finest is that at Exeter Cathedral, very lofty and the best specimen of medieval woodwork designed by Thomas of Whitney from 1312, remodelled in some ways with a seat of the reign of Elizabeth I, that survived the War by being dismantled and stored. Belfast St. Anne's Anglican Cathedral has two bishop's seats, possibly the only cathedral so endowed, as the bishop represents two dioceses.

It is interesting and perhaps surprising that the bishop, or archbishop, has no authority in the management of a cathedral; he is invited to participate, usually with courtesy, warmth and appreciation.

CEILING: the inside surface of the roof, usually flat and wooden, but not necessarily so. Search for those beautifully carved and painted, as at Peterborough from the 13th century and unique.

Peterborough and its imposing Early English Gothic West Front (façade) which, with its three enormous arches, is without architectural precedent and has this brilliant nave ceiling.

At Ely, the painted 19th century ceiling now restored is made of painted, wooden panels installed in 1858- 65 (previously one could see right up into the beams of the roof). It was typical of Victorian restorers to do things that they thought made a church more medieval-looking, even if there was no evidence that the church had really been like that in the Middle Ages.

Peterborough's nave ceiling

The ceiling at Chelmsford Cathedral

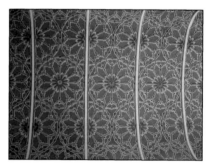

CHAIRS: (see also PEWS). In earlier times participants in services (the congregation) usually stood or kneeled on the stone floors during services, with some sitting in the stone archways at the sides of the nave. In the great cathedrals, the only place to sit was along the low stone shelf that ran along the side walls of the building, mainly for those who were too weak or ill to stand; hence the saying, *"The weak go to the wall"*.

Chairs have often replaced the earlier pews for more comfort and flexibility for all occasions as at Christ Church Oxford, as of March 2007, where all of the pews in the central crossing of the cathedral were removed, the floor restored and new chairs provided. The chairs are comfortable and the arrangement allows for much better visibility.

However, there are often difficulties: A newspaper report in 2009 states that the chapter at Ripon Cathedral would be deciding in principle whether to support the idea of chairs instead of pews for its congregation in the nave. (If the cathedral's controlling body decided to back the change, it would have to win final approval from the independent Fabric Advisory Committee which must be consulted by law on any major changes to cathedrals of the Church of England. Supporters of the chairs said they would be far more comfortable than the pews! Then a later report: *"Pews from Ripon Cathedral are to be turned into tables which will go on sale to the public to raise funds for the historic building when the benches are replaced by 300 new oak chairs. The decision has been taken to replace the pews to allow the nave to be cleared more easily for the growing number of events which are being held at the cathedral, such as education days for local schools."* Then under the heading: *"Pew'll have a hard time... for now!"* the scheme has been 'called in' for further consideration by the cathedral financial watchdog. The chapter had hoped to have all its chairs in place by Christmas, but now the Cathedral's Fabric Commission for England wants to ensure the new chairs will enhance and not detract from the nave's splendour. Orders for the new wooden framed chairs, upholstered in Ripon Red, the colour of the cathedral choir's cassocks, have been put on hold until approval has been given. Ancient or modern is the question?)

It looks as though modern won, for a further report says some of the pews, now made into tables, were being sold to Japan!

Similarly, a delegation from Bath Abbey (with similar pews to Ripon) recently visited St. Martin-in-the-Fields Church in London to look at excellent work that has been carried out there, and will look at the experiences of cathedrals such as York Minster, Salisbury and Winchester, where new comfortable seating has been installed. Any such change, for more comfort and however well-handled, is not without controversy – especially over cost at times of financial stringency. The most comfortable chairs tested by the writer are at Bradford Cathedral.

There are special chairs in some cathedrals, e.g., the St. Augustine's Chair used for the enthronement of archbishops in Canterbury Cathedral and named after the first archbishop, dating from the 13th century.

Unusually, Portsmouth Cathedral has a 1694 Corporation Chair used by the Lord Mayor when attending on official occasions. The Church of the Good Shepherd in Edinburgh has a 'Glastonbury' Chair used for special occasions.

These 'specials' are normally well- designed and embellished.

At Dunkeld Cathedral the idea of providing special chairs for use at weddings and other special occasions was approved. It was agreed that eight chairs should be specially commissioned and should first be comfortable but also should fit the atmosphere and surroundings of the cathedral. The design was therefore kept quite simple with no decoration and with the top rail reflecting the cusp detail of the pew ends and the seats without upholstery. The wood is unstained Argyll oak in keeping with the pews.

CHALICE (from the Latin calix) is a goblet or cup intended to hold a drink, and generally for drinking during a ceremony. In most Christian denominations, a chalice is a standing cup used to hold sacramental wine during the Eucharist or Holy Communion and is often made of precious metal, sometimes richly enamelled and jewelled.

Used regularly in St. Columb's Cathedral in Derry is a silver-gilt chalice, called the Promised Chalice, and paten, donated to the cathedral in 1613 when the 'Honourable Irish Society' that built the cathedral donated the vessels from London.

(Now on display in the National Museum of Ireland is an early example found in 1980 as part of a hoard of five liturgical vessels: the 8th-9th century *'Derrynaflan Chalice'* from Killenaule, the site of an early Irish abbey, in Co. Tipperary, Ireland. The chalice was found with a silver paten, a hoop that may have been a stand for the paten, a liturgical strainer and a bronze basin inverted over the other objects. The hoard was probably secreted during the turbulent 10th to 12th centuries, when Viking raids and turmoil caused valuables to be hidden).

The paten is the accompanying vessel, a small plate, usually made now of silver or gold, used to hold the Eucharistic bread which is to be consecrated, and generally used during the service itself; the paten is typically either a simple saucer-like plate or a low bowl. A smaller style paten will often have a depression that allows it to securely sit on top of the chalice. Most cathedrals will display the communion vessels in their treasury.

CHANCEL: the crucial space around the altar in a church, often enclosed, at the eastern end of a church for use primarily by the clergy and the choir, including the sanctuary: the two terms are often interchanged but the chancel is the greater part of the area. The sanctuary probably includes the 'Credence Table' (a small side table in the sanctuary of a Christian church which is used in the celebration of Eucharist and is usually placed near the wall of the sanctuary, and may be covered with a fine linen cloth. It is sometimes tended by an altar server, and contains on it the implements that are used in the Eucharistic celebration, which may include the bread and wine prior to their consecration, and a bowl and towel for the washing of hands).

In some churches, the pulpit and lectern may be in the chancel, but are normally in the Nave although in most cathedrals there is usually one lectern in the chancel.

The chancel is raised above the level of the nave where the congregation gathers and may be separated from the nave by a rood screen, a rail, or an open space.

Interestingly, the word *'chancel'* derives from the French usage of 'chancel' from a Late Latin word *'cancelli'* meaning 'lattice' that refers to the rood screen. The chancel arch is thus the arch which separates the chancel (sanctuary or choir) from the nave of a church. In medieval cathedrals the chancel was usually enclosed or blocked off from the nave by a screen, thus the chancel arch and screen are those separating the chancel from the nave or crossing. (An altar screen is that which is behind the altar to stop access from altar to the rear ambulatory, and to act as a decorative element behind the altar and its reredos.)

CHANTRY & CHAPEL: a chantry is described as an endowment for a priest to celebrate Mass for the founder's soul, usually in pre-Reformation times, so that a chantry chapel is that erected over a burial place within the building, and often ornately decorated and with an unusual history.

Winchester is famous for its chantry chapels, where daily Masses were said for the bishops buried within them: the two earliest are in the nave – that of William of Edington (bishop 1345-66) below the

Norman arcade, and William of Wykeham's soaring monument was built at the same time as his reconstructed nave. The remaining four chantry chapels stand in the retrochoir.

Beneath the tower-arch of the north transept is this Chapel of the Holy Sepulchre, that dates with colourful wall-paintings from about 1170 (as on previous page).

Chapel has several meanings, but mainly a chapel is a holy place or area of worship for Christians, sometimes small and attached to a larger institution such as a large church, a college, a hospital, a palace, a prison or a cemetery; sometimes large and unattached to another building. Architecturally, a chapel may be a part of a large church set aside for some specific use or purpose. All cathedrals have a chapel; most have a few as part of the building each with a separate altar and set aside for the purpose of prayer or meditation, or for a service such as Holy Communion. Chapels may be dedicated to a particular Saint, and 'Our Lady's Chapel' to the Virgin Mary is often the most prominent: Hereford, St. Alban's, Wells and York have exceptional examples. See also entry: 'royal peculiars'.

Bristol has two Lady chapels: one located just beyond the north transept of the church is called the Elder Lady chapel, built c.1220 as the first Gothic addition to the Norman church; the other, built during the early 1300s, is called the Eastern Lady chapel, and is traditionally situated behind the high altar. However, Bristol also has an adjacent civic Lord Mayor's Chapel that is unique: the only church in England owned by a local authority brought about by squabbles between city and cathedral in the 17th -18th centuries.

When Bristol's monasteries were closed, the canny council leapt at the chance to buy their properties. Among the gains was St. Mark's Hospital, which had its own chapel, so the city had it expensively repaired and fitted out, to be the riposte to the cathedral across the way. It is a beautiful church.

The chapels in the RC Cathedral at Westminster are especially noteworthy and attractive.

One of the finest chapels is in Scotland: the Thistle Chapel in the Cathedral of St. Giles Edinburgh, designed by Sir Robert Lorimer.

There is usually one chapel as a Chapel of Remembrance for lives lost in the Wars and linked with a particular local regiment or armed service, with Canterbury, Bradford, Guildford, Leicester and Sheffield having memorable regimental chapels.

Westminster Abbey is noted for its fine Royal Air Force Memorial Chapel. Lincoln Cathedral has a distinctive Airmen's Chapel of St. Michael.

(Occasionally a remembrance or lesser chapel is used as a storage place and if this occurs, one should complain to the cathedral or church authority.)

During the 13th century at Chichester, chapels were added to the nave aisles forming an unusual architectural feature, and making Chichester one of the widest English cathedrals. At Derby there is a linked but separate 'Chapel of St. Mary on the Bridge', an unsung treasure from the 14th century.

At Chester Cathedral in the north transept there is a 'Children and Young People's Chapel', and from the inside a view of the magnificent organ and its decorated pipes. Children are encouraged to write and post poems of their visit. One reads:

I sit here waiting
For hands and feet
To involve me in the music.
Five thousand shining pipes
Shoot air into the high roof space.
I can scream
Or I can groan like a rhino
I can make you cold
With blue-white notes
Or I can play rainbows.

CHAPTER & CHAPTER HOUSE: the appointed dean and his staff of canons are in charge of the administration of the cathedral and are known as 'The Chapter' – from the ancient time when the abbot of the monastery called a daily meeting of his brethren in the chapter house. Thus, a chapter house was built as a place for meetings of the clergy when a chapter from the Bible was read and so we have 'chapter meetings'. The chapter house is one of the attractive places in a cathedral, often with fine memorials and sometimes with important artefacts such as silverware, if not displayed in a treasury.

The octagonal chapter house at Lichfield Cathedral houses its greatest treasure, '*the Lichfield Gospels*', an 8th century illustrated manuscript. Also here in the vestibule from the north choir aisle to chapter house is a unique medieval '*pedilavium*' (a short corridor) where following the example of Jesus at the Last Supper, feet were washed on Maundy Thursday.

In Britain the chapter house is usually polygonal in shape (more than four sides and angles) with a slender central column that supports the roof. There is usually stone or wood benching around the inner walls on which the clergy sit to discuss business.

Particularly fine and noteworthy are those at Wells and at York (described as 'an octagonal box of delights' with carved corbels and Green Men sprouting oak leaves, and other strange creatures. York's chapter house has been used as a meeting house since its completion in 1286 even for Parliamentary sittings by Edwards I and II. It is reported that Charles I tried to summon his Parliament here during the Civil War but Parliament refused to respond to this summons).

That at Gloucester is important as William the Conqueror ordered the writing here of the Doomsday Survey of 1086.

At Bristol the chapter house and cloister are superb Norman architecture of 1165.

Worcester is 12th century, Southwell and Wells are 13th century; Chester has a noble room – an early English Gothic 1230-1265.

The chapter house at Salisbury houses the best preserved of the four remaining original exemplars of the 'Magna Carta' (Latin for 'Great Charter') – one of the most celebrated documents in English history. At the time it was the solution to a political crisis in medieval England but it has become recognised as a cornerstone of liberty influencing much of the civilised world.

In Lincoln, at the Parliament of 1301 held in the chapter house by Edward I, he declared his fourth son Edward of Caernarvon, the First English Prince of Wales, who later became Edward II. (The oak chair here is said to have been the chair used by Edward I, on this occasion, and arms of the chair are carved with the leopards of England and the lilies of France. In 1536 the chapter house was used for meetings by the church and the members of the Lincolnshire Uprising against rules from Henry VIII. It ended up that about a hundred people were eventually executed including the Lord Lieutenant. Many of the windows of the chapter house here depict scenes from the uprising and were made in Victorian times by Clayton and Bell.)

Westminster Abbey's chapter house from around 1225, one of the oldest buildings in London, has been the scene of special repair, a £3million, 18-month project completed in 2010, where 20 master carvers and stonemasons have repaired badly-weathered gargoyles, stone floral friezes, flying buttresses and stained glass windows, that include 32 new stone heads across eight pinnacles, and four new gargoyles. The new heads are portraits of people involved in the project including masons, architects and members of the clergy!

CHASUBLE is a sleeveless vestment (probably from French and Latin of a hooded cloak) of the celebrant at Mass or Eucharist usually worn over the surplice. See also robes and vestments.

CHEVET is a style of construction that creates an ambulatory and radiating chapels at the eastern end of a church.

CHEVRON is seen in a Norman building, the actual ornament shaped like a 'V', and known as a 'zig-zag' on the columns. Durham Cathedral and Dunfermline Abbey have noted examples on their columns.

CHOIR, or more ancient name *Quire*, is the place for the Singers and forms 'a church within a church' and is the place where prayer and worship are offered, giving the marvellous opportunity at Sung Evensong to sit alongside the choir in the quire. The four stalls at the corners are normally allocated to four senior residential clergy responsible for the management and worship. Other stalls, dedicated to and named after saints, are allocated to other members of the cathedral chapter.

At Salisbury, for example, the named clergy were known as 'prebends', the estates and farms given to the cathedral to provide an income for the clergy. When the income was taken away from Salisbury and other ancient cathedrals to provide income for cathedrals in growing cities such as Liverpool and Manchester, stalls were allocated to senior clergy as 'honorary canons', and some allocated to distinguished lay men and women, known as 'lay canons'.

The bishop's seat or throne is usually at the east end of the quire near to the sanctuary and its high altar, the focal point of the cathedral.

Much of the woodwork in quires is original and outstanding. Most medieval cathedrals have beautifully carved stalls in the quire, and at Chester the quality of oak carving from 1380 is exceptional: each stall is topped with an elaborately carved canopy set above a row of small corbels – this area is so richly carved with an array of religious artefacts, animals, birds and grotesque figures that it is quite overwhelming.

Carlisle also has some of the finest medieval stalls with scenes of the life of the 5th century St. Augustine of Hippo (now Annaba in Algeria) who happens to be patron saint of brewers and whose voluminous writings had a profound effect on the development of Christianity and the Church.

The Salisbury Quire features the largest and earliest complete set of choir stalls with intricate carvings and a magnificent selection of 'misericords'. Below each seat is a magnificently carved 'misericord' (derived from the Latin 'misericordia' – pity).

Examine the tip-up seats, where possible, where monks and nuns would perch and rest, and underneath are beautiful

carvings, often of fables and animals – in Salisbury of foliage. On the arms of the stalls are birds and animals, often a unique mix of woodwork from the 13th century, carvings partly medieval and some 19th century, with the canopies made, remarkably, between 1912-1925. This shown has an owl depicted.

See also 'retrochoir'.

CHOIRBOOK is an illustrated manuscript. The Eton Choirbook (MS 178 in Eton College Cambridge) is a richly illuminated manuscript collection of English sacred music composed during the late 15th century. It was one of very few collections of Latin liturgical music to survive the Reformation (when the enormous majority of music from the 15th and early 16th centuries was destroyed in the Dissolution of the Monasteries by Henry VIII) and originally contained music by 24 different composers; however, many of the pieces are damaged or incomplete. The Eton Choirbook was compiled between approximately 1500 and 1505 for use at Eton College; its present binding dates from the mid 16th century. 126 folios remain of the original 224, including the index. In the original, there were 93 separate compositions; however only 64 remain either complete or in part. It is one of three large choirbooks surviving from early Tudor England (the others are the Lambeth Choirbook and the Caius Choirbook).

(Only two compositions of Richard Hygons – 1435-1509 composer at Wells Cathedral – are known to survive: a two-voice setting of the Gaude virgo mater Christi, which appears on a single surviving leaf of a choir book from Wells, and in the Eton Choirbook the famous Salve Regina – unique among English music of the period. The complexity and craftsmanship shown in Hygon's Salve Regina has suggested that the musical standards at Wells Cathedral at the end of the 15th century were high, and matched those of musical centres in Europe).

A special *'Choirbook for the Queen'* is to be published by the Canterbury Press in November 2011, the inspirational idea of Robert Ponsonby (former Controller of BBC Radio 3) to create a latter-day equivalent of 'The Eton Choirbook', the anthology of Tudor Music produced between 1500 and 1505 in honour of King Henry VII. Comprising two volumes, the new Choirbook contains 45 anthems to reflect the best of choral music by the living British composers in the 21st century. There is a Choirbook Trust: www.thechoirbooktrust.org.uk

CIVIL WAR (English) was a conflict between Charles I and Parliament in the 17th century resulting in much damage to cathedrals and abbeys. In September 1643, Parliament decided to rid churches of anything which they believed was connected with the Pope and Roman Catholicism.

For example, the Puritans in Norwich believed the cathedral contained many such ornaments and ideas. They objected to the colours, ornaments, monuments, brasses, painted glass, images and carvings: 1643 therefore proved to be a significant year in the life of its cathedral when an angry mob entered the cathedral and caused much panic and destruction. Some of the damage may still be seen today with graffiti inscribed by Parliamentary musketeers, a musket ball still lodged in Bishop Goldwell's tomb, and heads of statues missing and also, incredibly, the despenser reredos (a painting on wood used to decorate the altar) was hidden during the Civil War by being turned upside down and used as a table – in this way it survived!

Towards the end of the 16th century, Durham Cathedral was severely vandalised and was again in 1650 when Cromwell imprisoned some 4,000 Scots.

At Peterborough all the stained glass windows, the high altar and medieval choir stalls, and all the monuments and memorials of the cathedral were destroyed by Cromwell's soldiers in 1643. The royalist city of York was besieged by Parliamentarian troops but their general, the Yorkshireman Lord Fairfax, ordered that York Minster should be saved. See also Appendix D.

CLERESTORY, or clear storey, is found in an aisled building: the upper storey as part of the main wall below the eaves and above the top of the aisled roof, pierced with windows to give light to the interior.

CLOCKS were sparse in medieval churches when services were announced by the ring of bells.

The cathedral clock in the north transept of Wells Cathedral is an astronomical clock.

(In 1388, Bishop Ralph Erghum moved from Salisbury to Wells: previously Bishop of Salisbury, from 1375 to 1388, he had installed a clock at Salisbury in 1386 and may have brought his clockmakers with him to Wells. The two clocks are almost identical in construction. The surviving

mechanism at Wells, dated between 1386 and 1392, was replaced in the 19th century, and was eventually moved to the Science Museum in London, where it continues to operate. The dial represents the view of the universe, with sun and moon revolving round a central fixed earth. Above the clock and to the right is a figure, known as Jack Blandifers, who hits bells with a hammer held in his right hand and by hitting his heels on two bells hung beneath him.

A set of jousting knights also chase each other every 15 minutes. Another dial (also shown) is mounted on the outside wall, driven from the same mechanism and first installed in the 14th or 15th centuries, but restored a number of times. In August 2010, the current Keeper of the Clock, Paul Fisher, announced his retirement that will end the practice of winding the clock by hand: the cathedral has decided to fit an electric motor to wind the clock!)

The oldest surviving mechanical clock in Britain, and probably in the world, was installed in Salisbury Cathedral in 1386.

(There was a mechanical clock working in Milan by 1335. It is the first for which there is firm evidence although there are suggestions that there were some mechanical clocks in existence before 1300. The Salisbury Clock is not as advanced as the one at Wells. There is no clock face; rather, the clock rings a chime of bells on the hour; that was intended to summon bishops to prayer. Designed to ring the clock in the bell tower (long since demolished), the right side of the clock is the part that keeps the time and the left side was the side that rang the bell. It also has a small dial that indicates the hour.

Rediscovered in the 1930s when it was described as "a pile of junk in one of the cathedral's roof spaces", it now resides in the cathedral north aisle and is still in working order – though the side that rings only does the motions and has no bell to ring).

An astronomical clock was installed in the north transept of York Minster in 1955 as a memorial, dedicated on 1st November 1955, by HRH The Duke of Edinburgh, to honour the 18,000 airmen who died whilst serving with the Royal Air Force, Women's Auxiliary Air Force and the Air Forces of the Commonwealth in Yorkshire, Durham and Northumberland during the Second World War.

The Astronomical Clock at York Minster

(The clock demonstrates the precise position of the sun and the 'fixed' stars in relation to the centre of York at all times of the day and throughout the year, and is accurate to within one minute. The clock and its mechanism are contained within a walnut wood frame designed by Professor A E Richardson, President of the Royal Academy).

Exeter has a clock from 1484 in a space in its north transept under the tower, and also where there are wooden doorways; the one under the clock has a round hole that allows a cat to enter the tower to deter mice. Keep a lookout!

CLOISTER means 'to enclose or to shut up' thus the term 'cloistered' – secluded or sheltered as perhaps in a convent or monastic house, monastic life or seclusion. The cloisters were known as a covered place for walking, often round a quadrangle (a four-sided court) with a wall on the outer side, and a colonnade or windows on the inner side, usually constructed as a covered way around a grassed area but not a burial ground: in monastic times cloisters were used by monks and nuns as a place of prayer and meditation when not actually in the church. Nowadays older relics and

memorials are often displayed in the cloisters.

That at Salisbury is shown left: that at Gloucester is also outstanding complete with lavatorium (from 'lavare' – to wash) and on the west walk with carrels where monks studied and wrote.

At Chester many of the monastic buildings from the ancient Benedictine Abbey have been remarkably preserved. The original cloisters, although rebuilt during the first half of the 16th century and restored at the beginning of the 20th century, are a reminder of the important part they played in monastic life. The monks' dining room is still used regularly; as is the superb chapter house.

Several, as at Norwich and Worcester, have famous 'bosses'.

St. Andrew's Metropolitan Cathedral in Glasgow is to create an imaginative new apse and cloister garden as part of intensive renovation.

CLOSE is a square or enclosed area very near to the cathedral where the staff of the cathedral may live. The most famous close is probably that at Salisbury where the late Edward Heath MP, Prime Minister, had his home. Here the imposing buildings provide a journey through history: 'Mompesson House' is a Queen Anne special from 1701 (featured in the film *Sense and Sensibility*), and nearby is 'The Wardrobe', dating from the 13th century and used as a clothing store by bishops from the 14th century, now a museum of the Rifles regiments. See also Lichfield, Lincoln, Peterborough and Winchester for a particular close.

Another title is the 'precinct' (space enclosed by walls or other boundaries at a place of worship) where at Gloucester Cathedral there are buildings not only from the 17th and 18th centuries, but also from the 12th and 13th centuries when the initial abbey was built.

COLUMN is a cylindrical, slightly tapered pillar supporting some part of the building, usually in three parts: base, shaft and capital.

COMMUNION: a body professing one branch of Christian faith, for example the Anglican Communion. The word also means 'sharing', participation as in the service of Holy Communion; and 'fellowship' especially between branches of the Catholic Church.

CONFESSIONAL: In Roman Catholic and some Anglican cathedrals and churches, a small box structure or enclosure in which a priest hears confessions from a kneeling penitent.

CONSISTORY COURT: a council of pope and cardinals, a Lutheran clerical board, a court of Presbyters, or an Anglican bishop's court for ecclesiastical causes and offences, so it is common in several denominations. It is a court under the jurisdiction of a bishop where misdemeanours of clergy and parishes can be heard, and judged. The actual court preserved at Leicester Cathedral is very notable and prominent within the nave; that at Chester with oak screens, seats and table dates from 1636; Derby has a high canopied seat in a railed enclosure from 1634, and also a relic of 'the Derby Plank' from its court found during repairs in 1948, with painted scene of starry sky, moon and sun, perhaps representing 'the Last Judgement' found in such courts.

CORBEL is a stone block projecting from a wall to carry the end of a beam or roof-truss, and often carved with grotesque human and animal figures. (See also gargoyle.)

Hereford's Green Lion Corbels

Illustrated is a corbel head at the entrance to the crypt at Canterbury, dating from the mid-12th century, and a display of corbels at Hereford.

Said to be the smallest ancient cathedral in Britain, St. Asaph in Wales has medieval nave pillars, completely unadorned and with no capitals, contrasting vividly with the luxurious 19th century oak-ribbed ceiling springing from decorative corbels.

CORONA: primarily a small circle of light around the sun or moon, but in a building a circular chandelier hung from the roof. The Corona in a church is often symbolic of the crown of thorns and at Canterbury is the total east-end named after the severed crown of Thomas Becket whose shrine it was built to contain.

Blackburn RC Cathedral has a steel corona of the crown of thorns. At Lancaster is the '*Corona Lucis*', the Crown of Light, noteworthy over its altar.

At Llandaff is this modern great Corona that dominates and unfortunately blocks much of the view of the cathedral from the west entrance. However it houses some of the pipes of the organ.

(In 1941 during World War II the cathedral was severely damaged when a landmine was dropped near it during the Cardiff Blitz, blowing the roof off the nave, south aisle and

chapter house. The top of the spire also had to be reconstructed and there was also damage to the organ. Of British cathedrals, only Coventry was damaged more. Major restoration was carried out and the building returned to use in June 1958. The Welch Regiment memorial chapel was constructed, and Sir Jacob Epstein created the figure of Christ in Majesty which is suspended above the nave on a concrete arch designed by George Pace.)

Liverpool Anglican Cathedral has a corona gallery; of its two pipe organs, the grand organ is the second largest organ in Britain (that at the Royal Albert Hall having one additional stop!) and is the largest church organ, and its *'Trompette Militaire'* of 1997 is located on the Corona Gallery.

CROSIER, or crozier, is the hooked staff or crook that symbolises the pastoral office of the bishop. In Western Christianity, the crosier has a curved or hooked top, shaped like a shepherd's crook. A bishop/head of church bears this staff as *'shepherd of the flock of God'*, particularly the community under his canonical jurisdiction, but any bishop, whether or not assigned to a functional diocese, also uses a crosier when conferring sacraments and presiding at liturgies. Crosiers are often made of fine metal, or at least gilded or silver-plated. They may also be made of wood, though this is more common of the crosier carried by an abbot than of a bishop.

At St. David's Cathedral in Wales, a bishops' crosier at least 600 years old is held in its treasury (along with coins from the reign of Edward III -1327/37) and also in its library are books from 1505 and the leaf of a manuscript of Exodus from the 1620 Edition of the Welsh Bible. There is much symbolism attached to the Crosier and it is worth searching for its historical context.

Is the bishop's crosier named after the natural fern 'crozier'? (right)

(It was reported in the Irish Times on 22.6.2000 that an Ellen O'Carroll of the Archaeological Development Services in Ireland discovered a rare 6th century bishop's crosier stuck vertically in the mud as she surveyed in advance of peat harvesting in Offaly county near Ferbane. The crozier, now broken into several segments, was originally about 1.25 meters long with a 25mm diameter. It appears to have been carved out of a single branch or stem of cherry wood. The crozier is believed to be the earliest one discovered in Ireland. Surprisingly, the crook is crafted to enclose a Greek cross and the tip of the crozier is "stepped and pointed". It was discovered next to a pathway of split oak planks dated to AD

596. The site is only ten miles from the ancient monastic centre at Clonmacnois.

There are many stories about St. Patrick: we are told that often Patrick baptised hundreds on a single day. On such a day Aengus, a prince of Munster, was baptised. Patrick got out his book and began to look for the place of the baptismal rite but his crozier got in the way. The bishop's crozier often has a spike at the bottom end, probably to allow the bishop to set it into the ground to free his hands. So, when Patrick fumbled searching for the right spot in the book so that he could baptise Aengus, he absent-mindedly stuck his crosier into the ground just beside him – and accidentally through the foot of Aengus! Patrick, concentrating on the sacrament, never noticed what he had done and proceeded with the baptism. The prince never cried out, nor moaned; he simply went very white. Patrick poured water over his bowed head at the simple words of the rite. Then it was completed and Aengus was a Christian. Patrick turned to take up his crozier and was horrified to find that he had driven it through the prince's foot! "But why didn't you say something?. Your foot is bleeding and you'll be lame...." Then Aengus said in a low voice that he thought having a spike driven through his foot was part of the ceremony. He then said, "Christ shed His blood for me, and I am glad to suffer a little pain at baptism to be like Our Lord.")

CROSS is the main sign of Christianity symbolising the death of Jesus. It is often used in processionals within a church and outdoors for witness and at special festivals. The cross is probably the most frequent sign or artefact within a church building, always on an altar, above the pulpit, on the lectern, often within the stained glass. It is also part of the Agnus Dei, (the lamb with a cross) usually in stained glass. Many crosses were destroyed at the Reformation, and during the Civil War by Cromwell's army.

Llandaff Cathedral stands on one of the oldest Christian sites in Britain: in the 6th century St. Dyfrig founded a community close to the ford where the Roman road crossed the river Taff. Nothing remains of the original church but a Celtic cross that stood nearby can still be seen near the door of the chapter house.

This outdoor cross at Wells Cathedral is much larger than normal and larger than other related memorial crosses here.

This photograph (courtesy of Cornell University Library) is of Hereford Cathedral illustrating the famous screen by Sir George Gilbert Scott with its cross, pulpit and lectern.

CROSSING is an important part of a cathedral. It is the square space formed by the intersection of nave and transepts, the centre of the cross-shape of the building, and under the high section of the tower: the space where the nave, transepts and quire meet.

Many important cathedrals have lofty central towers over the crossing as at Canterbury, Durham, Gloucester, Lincoln, St. Alban's, Salisbury and York Minster, with Ely having the very famous 'lantern' tower. (See also spire, steeple and tower.)

At St. Giles in Edinburgh, the nave and chancel are about the same length, so the crossing and the tower are in the centre of the church rather than towards its eastern end, and the transepts are no longer than the aisles of the nave and chancel are wide. This gives a very broad rectangular space in which the transepts are not particularly dominant.

CRYPT is an underground cell (from the Greek 'kruptos' – a hidden place), an undercroft, or a vault especially used as a burial place beneath a church, usually without windows; although in the crypt at Canterbury that has windows, there are now chapels. Many were very large to allow pilgrims to meet, and crypts are often used as an exhibition space.

Notable examples are:

St. Paul's London, said to be the largest in Europe, with the 'Order of the British Empire Chapel', and distinguished memorials including that of Lord Nelson, and a fine shop and restaurant.

York has a permanent museum that contains many historic treasures including early Norman columns decorated with geometric designs similar to those at Durham

Cathedral. Though they appear solid, they are in fact rubble-filled shells. Canterbury has the largest 12th century crypt in the world; Gloucester an 11th century with heavy squat columns.

The Saxon crypt at Ripon houses the cathedral's treasury.

Winchester's crypt is entered from the north transept, is Norman and regularly flooded in winter; seen here with an Antony Gormley statue.

Antony Gormley Statue

St. Magnus Cathedral in Kirkwall, Orkney, is the only cathedral to have a dungeon, known to have held men and women imprisoned even in the 18th century. It is also the most northernmost cathedral in Britain and also the only cathedral owned by the local council and managed by the Church of Scotland – the Protestant Church that does not have bishops but maintains a few historic cathedrals.

It has also another unique feature with a series of 17th century stone 'grave-markers' with carved reminders of mortality (coffins, hour-glasses, skulls and other bones) fixed on the walls of each aisle with the historic writings translated on plaques for the benefit of visitors.

Its north aisle contains also a unique wooden grave-marker called a 'mort brod'.

Example of 'Mort Brod' and stone Grave Marker in St. Magnus Cathedral, Orkney

ELEVEN

DISCIPLE. In the history of Christianity, a disciple was the student of Jesus during his ministry. When Jesus attracted a large following, the term 'disciple' was used to refer specifically to 'the Twelve', an inner circle of men whose number perhaps represented the 12 tribes of Israel. Appendix C, *'Disciples and Apostles'*, gives their names and key roles. The word *'disciple'* is used today usually as a method of identification for those who seek to learn from the teachings of Jesus. Visitors to cathedrals may see a copy of the famous painting *'The Sermon on the Mount'* by Carl Heinrich Bloch: the mount being Mount Zion with Jesus preaching to his disciples.

DOG-TOOTH MOULDING has, apparently, nothing to do with the animal, but is an ornamental stone moulding consisting of a row of pyramidal projections each carved into four leaves; used in English cathedrals during the 13th century, as at Salisbury.

DOME, sometimes named a rotunda, is a convex roof over a square, circular or octagonal space, as noteworthy in the complex dome of St. Paul's London. This comprises three main sections: an inner decorated dome seen from below, then an invisible brick cone that carries the tremendous weight

of the stone 'lantern' above, and then the external dome of timber on top, and covered with lead.

TWELVE

EMBROIDERY is an ornament with needlework – sometimes described unfortunately as an 'inessential ornament' as it often covers up an item such as an historic wooden or stone altar. Embroidery is used to produce banners to be carried in processions or displayed on the pillars of the church and on altar frontals, lectern markers and pulpit falls covering the pulpit's book-rest. Embroidered cloths are an ancient tradition and a major feature of medieval decorations, in the home and in church. However in Scotland, the coming of Presbyterianism had the effect of banishing most of the colour in churches, but in recent times this has changed. Now, we see pulpit falls, frontals for Communion tables, pictures, banners, even parts of the robes, decorated or embellished in different, colourful ways.

Every cathedral and abbey has a supply and most embroideries are of exceptional quality of design especially on altar frontals. Embroidery is mentioned in the Bible in Exodus 38, Judges V and Psalm 45.

The medieval word 'tappisser' was given to workers generally in handicrafts.

Exeter is especially known for its fine embroidery and the best-known group is probably the 'Exeter Cathedral of Tapisers' with their 'Brightest Array': a suitable title for the skilled work on altar cloths and frontals, kneelers and vestments and especially on a set of 'rondels' with the theme of the history not only of Exeter but national, and placed on the plinths on sides of the nave.

(A little bit of Lancashire humour creeps in at Exeter Cathedral, as its 'Oldham Chantry' houses the tomb of Bishop Oldham, founder of Manchester Grammar School. Oldham is pronounced by locals as 'Owldom', so the altar kneelers have a pattern of owls copied from the wall stonework!)

Even as the construction of Liverpool Anglican Cathedral commenced in 1904, a number of remarkable ladies formed the Cathedral Embroidery Association to much scepticism about their possible standard of work, and made not only a complete set of altar frontals but a set of 44 surplices of high standard, before the cathedral was consecrated.

EPISTLE & GOSPEL are books of the Holy Bible and from them emanate the terms 'epistle side' meaning the south side of a chancel from which the epistle was read, and 'gospel side' the north side of a chancel from which the gospel is read. These 'side-terms' seem out of date now as the epistle from the New Testament of the Bible, along with a lesson from the Old Testament, is usually read from the lectern, while the gospel is usually read with a little more ceremony from a special 'Book of the Gospels' in the centre of the chancel or aisle.

EUCHARIST is the central act of Christian worship in which bread and wine are consecrated and consumed; also from the Greek word 'eukharistia' meaning thanksgiving:

thus the services of Eucharist or Holy Communion, and as noted later the 'Mass'. It is interesting to note that during the 2009 outbreak of Swine Fever, some churches had refrained from serving the wine to avoid any risk of infection, emphasising that the service of consecrated bread alone is justified.

THIRTEEN

FACADE is the principal front, or face, usually the west front of a building. Wells Cathedral has one of, if not, the finest of English cathedrals' facades, but see also west front.

The magnificent west facade of Wells Cathedral.

Rochester also has a fine Romanesque facade contrasting with a modern fresco completed in 2004 by a Russian iconographer. An interesting story of Gothic church facades can be seen on the following website: www.buildinghistory.org

FAN-VAULTING is the latest and elaborate phase of English Gothic vaulting, attractive but perhaps over-complicated in design. Sherborne Abbey is famous for its fan vaulting, majestic tower and superb flying buttresses. Technically, the FAN VAULT is described as a sophisticated form of barrel vault built of cut stone, consisting of inverted conoids (cone-shaped) decorated with a fan of purely decorative surface ribs, often with pendant bosses.

Fan vaults appear at first over small spaces. The earliest known structural examples are those of the 14th century in the cloister of Gloucester Cathedral. Bath Abbey was built 'by a dream': the dreamer Oliver King, bishop and secretary to Henry VII who dreamed of angels climbing a ladder with a voice telling him "Let a King restore the church" so he had the Norman abbey pulled down and began a new 'cathedral' in 1499, but the nave was not completed until Victorian times with the resulting fan vaulting described as 'a superb rhythmic unity'. On a large scale the fan vault remained exceptional, associated with especially prestigious buildings in the Perpendicular style of the end of the 15th and early 16th centuries.

FLOOR TILING: a revival in the 19th century of the use of tiles with burnt-in wax paint, known as 'encaustic', revived what was a medieval practice. Several medieval tiles have survived and may be viewed in the pavements in  cathedrals, such as the floor tiles in Lichfield Cathedral library dating from the 13th century, or at Winchester as shown.

Even more spectacular is the *Cosmati pavement* in Westminster Abbey, described under mosaic.

FLYING BUTTRESS: see Buttress.

FONT is a receptacle to contain holy water used for the Sacrament of Baptism. It is unclear whether this word links with fount as a spring, source or fountain, or as a reservoir of oil in a lamp. (Interestingly the terms in printing of 'fount' and 'font' mean a set of type of the same face and size). The font in a cathedral or church is usually close to the entry, because baptism is the sacrament of entrance to the Christian community. The Canon Law of the Church of England does state, *"the font shall stand as near to the principal entrance as conveniently may be."* The font is normally in stone or marble and sculpted, often with a pelican in its piety (plucking the blood from its breast to feed its young). Some fonts have a wooden cover suspended by a chain.

St. Mary's Cathedral, Edinburgh has three fonts – one near the entrance, one in a side chapel, and a wooden portable font placed near the organ chamber.

St. Paul's London has a main font in the north transept, and a smaller one in the chapel of the 'Order of the British Empire' in its crypt, as members of the Order have the opportunity for a family christening, or a wedding in the chapel.

One of the finest fonts, as here, in marble is at Lichfield.

Other notable fonts are at Bath Abbey (1710), Canterbury, Hereford, Portsmouth, Wells and Winchester. Derby has a new font from 1974 of marble from the Aegean.

Brecon's Norman font, the largest in Britain, is also unique for its stone crest with 30 cups. Northern Ireland's Down Cathedral houses a massive 11th century granite font discovered in use as a watering trough around 1930 that may have been the base of an early stone cross, and of course nearby is the reputed burial-place of St. Patrick.

Blackburn's modern font is unique-shaped as an egg and placed in the south transept that was to have been the entrance. Without a window, there is space for an adjacent major sculpture of 'Christ the Worker' – a neat combination of birth to adulthood.

This beautiful modern font at St. Magnus Cathedral has a marble band surrounding the bowl of the font and inlaid with 29 polished stones brought by children from each parish and island of Orkney to mark the 850th anniversary of the cathedral.

Salisbury Cathedral has the most recent new Font described as a Modern Treasure and perhaps the most significant addition to the fabric of an English Cathedral in recent years: the Cathedral's first permanent font for over 150 years with living streams of water from its four corners where the surrounding windows are reflected in the font.

FRESCOE is a method of painting in water-colour laid on the wall or ceiling before the plaster is dry: murals are painted apparently after the plaster is dry. The frescoe at Carlisle depicts the lives of St. Anthony, St. Augustine and St. Cuthbert; other key ones are at Canterbury and Lincoln – especially a modern one of 1958 in the Russell Chantry Chapel, and at Rochester and St. Albans.

FOURTEEN

GALILEE is a pronounced type of porch or chapel at the west end of a cathedral as at Durham (Norman with remarkable carvings) and Ely, and often used as a chapel for women or penitents. Interestingly this might derive from the Latin *'galeria'*, or even from the Bible. In St. Mark, chapter 16, verse 7 we read: *"He goeth before you into Galilee; there shall ye see Him,"* suggesting a meeting place, thus the name. At Newport, Wales, the present building has sections that date from pre-Norman times: in the 9th century the wooden church formerly on the site was rebuilt in stone and part of this building is now incorporated into St. Woolos Cathedral as the Galilee chapel now at the west end of the cathedral.

GARGOYLE: a grotesque spout usually in the form of a human or animal mouth, head, or body, projecting from a gutter especially of a Gothic building to carry water clear of the wall: some are more modern and some are found in the interior with all the characteristics but not as spouts, so presumably they are not, strictly, gargoyles. Note also the term 'beak-head' that is a grotesque ornament used in English Renaissance architecture in rows along the line of mouldings, suggesting a head with a beak, or a cat's head if the tongue hangs out. Gloucester Cathedral, having restored its north transept and south aisle, is now working on the

This Gargoyle is at St. Giles Cathedral in Edinburgh.

replacement of 13 gargoyles, based on Psalm 148, all new and designed by its master mason.

The Lincoln Imp is a famous and distinctive type of decoration in Lincoln Cathedral:

(The devil was out for a ride on the wind when he saw the new cathedral being built on top of a hill in Lincoln. Of an inquisitive nature he looked into the church, sat on top of one of the columns and went to sleep... never to wake again. He was turned to stone and can be seen 'resting' in the angel choir at the east end of the cathedral.)

Now restored, as in the photograph, it is said he grins at people who solemnly gaze upon him – miniatures are sold by the score at the cathedral.

Chester Cathedral also has its own imp. On the northern aisle of the nave at Chester, to the side of one of the large windows, sits the 'Chester Imp: a charming little figure in chains, carved by one of the medieval monks to protect the church from evil spirits.

GATEHOUSE: normally found in the wall that surrounds the Close as a guard to protect the inhabitants, and may be viewed at Bristol, Canterbury, Norwich, Salisbury, Wells and Worcester, and at St. David's Wales (with a bell tower).

GOSPEL is a writing that describes the life of Jesus (from Old English, god spell – good news). The word is used mainly to refer to the four gospels in the Holy Bible: *Matthew, Mark, Luke and John*, reported to have been written between AD 65 and 80, and apparently originally untitled, quoted anonymously in the first half of the 2nd century (i.e., 100–150), but the names by which they are now known were identified around the year 180.

A reading from a gospel is normally included in each service at a cathedral. See also Bible and disciples.

GOTHIC ART was a medieval art movement that developed in France out of Romanesque art in the mid-12th century, led by the similar development of Gothic architecture. It spread to all of Western Europe, but took over art more completely north of the Alps, never quite effacing more classical styles in Italy. In many areas, especially in Germany, Late Gothic art continued well into the 16th century and included sculpture, panel painting, stained glass, fresco and illuminated manuscript. The earliest Gothic art was monumental sculpture, on the walls of cathedrals and abbeys. Christian art showed stories of the Old and New Testaments often side by side and the lives of saints were often depicted. See also under architecture.

GREEN MAN: Often hidden, a strange figure sometimes surrounded by leaves, gazes down on visitors. Called the Green Man, he is not a gargoyle, but a sculpture created by

the mason or apprentice, expressing feelings of humour, tranquillity, or even fear and menace. Many medieval churches have a Green Man, often the only sculpture to have survived the Reformation. They were almost certainly symbols, but perhaps they were sculpted to indicate a mood, someone or something alive amongst the fabric; often sculpted high up in position or made in a workroom and fitted later.

They are a carver's skill, in wood and stone, and rarely found in illuminated books – although apparently copied from illuminated manuscripts – but occasionally in stained glass. The first is thought to have appeared in England in the 12th century although were witnessed earlier in Italy from the first century AD.

Oxford's grandest college, Christ Church, is a centre of Green Man imagery: foliate-faces loom from walls, columns, roof bosses and door surrounds. Especially beautiful carvings can be seen on the 13th century tomb of St. Frideswide in Christ Church Cathedral. Made in 1289, the shrine is the cathedral's oldest monument, and shows three serene stone faces peeping out from behind exquisitely carved foliage. Images of a Green Woman or perhaps of St. Frideswide herself?

See also 'bosses' and 'misericords' for Green Men.

Mike Harding – author, poet and comedian – has a fine set of *'Little Books'* including *'A Little Book of the Green Man'* (see Further Reading). As he so aptly describes, Green Men can be found in many forms, for example: 'Angels and Green Men' as at Rosslyn Chapel, Edinburgh, where there are thought to be 103 Green Men; a 'Green Man in Anguish' and possibly an 'Anglo-Indian foliate head' at Beverley Minster; 'Jack and the May King'; a 'Snake Head and Lion Head', with a jolly lion at Hereford Cathedral; 'Golden Heads on High' as at Tewkesbury Abbey that has a great number of Green Men, some re-gilded; and roof bosses as in many cathedrals.

There is a 'Green Misericord' at Southwell Minster and in its chapter house a series associated with amazing leaf sculpture from between 1280 and 1300; the craftsmanship mainly on the leaves including hemp, hop, ivy, maple, nettle and rose. At Exeter Cathedral on a stately column is a fine figure of the Virgin Mary who stands on a Green Man that is the source of the leafy sculpture that surrounds her. Green Men are often found in this subservient position on the base of sculptures. In the vault at Rochester Cathedral is a rough-bearded face that glares down, perhaps a reminder of savage fellows who threatened peasants in the forests.

At Ely the masons had a head for heights, for a carving was created 70 feet (20 metres) high and is of a sinister face hidden among foliage. At Exeter however, a green devil is to be found beneath a misericord, with tongue protruding wickedly, and horns projecting into oak branches.

Dragons with foliage appear in 10th century manuscripts with lions becoming later the more popular form of animal head; one wickedly colourful form at Canterbury is rather like a dragon; perhaps modelled on a human head with tongue hanging out: rude or just panting? Later, the lion became more of a jovial imp than a menacing form.

From the 18th century more 'human' type Green Men are to be found on ironwork, on gates and screens, such as at Tewkesbury Abbey Gage Gates and on a screen at St. Paul's London.

More recently, even artists have used the Green Man image in paintings, for example Mary Fedden in her painting of a harvest festival with a fully clothed Green Man with foliage and holding a hymn-book standing next to a singing couple.

GROIN VAULT: formed from two intersecting barrel vaults (the groins are the edges of the intersections). They are built of heavy rubble masonry and so need adequate support. They were used in the large crypts introduced by the Normans below their new abbeys and cathedrals, where the space was divided into a series of small bays by numerous columns, as at Canterbury, Worcester and Gloucester.

FIFTEEN

HYMNS are a type of song, usually religious, specifically written for the purpose of praise, adoration or prayer, and typically addressed to a deity or deities, or to a prominent figure. The word *hymn* derives from Greek *hymnos* – 'a song of praise'.

A large number of hymn-books were in use within the Church of England by the mid-Victorian period, and a chance meeting in a railway carriage by two clergymen led apparently to the formation of a group of supporters who considered the production of a single hymnal and founded a board called 'The Proprietors'. This was with the aim of donation of profits to appropriate charities, or to subsidise less wealthy parishes for the cost of the books.

The first *'Hymns Ancient & Modern'* was published in 1860, and became firmly established world-wide. It is estimated that since its inception, in excess of 165 million copies of Hymns Ancient & Modern have been sold. There are now revised versions and other types of hymn-book in the various cathedrals and churches. For example, in 2000 Hymns Ancient & Modern Ltd, through its subsidiary, the Canterbury Press, published a new hymnal called *'Common Praise'*. There is a website of the charity – www.hymnsam. co.uk – and also a website database: www.stmarysbaldock. fsnet.co.uk/hymns

I.H.S is the symbol often found in stained glass and on crosses, said to be a contraction of the name of Jesus. It is probably the initials from Jesus Hominum Salvator – 'Jesus Saviour of Mankind'. Records show also that the Emperor Constantine suggested I(n) H(oc) S(igho) as the sign *'I will conquer'*.

KEYSTONE is the important wedge-shaped central stone of an arch on which the arch depends.

SIXTEEN

LANCET is an early Gothic window with a sharply pointed head. See the earlier note on styles of architecture as the term 'Lancet style' succeeded the name for the Early English phase. Examples are seen notably in Lichfield and also in Bristol (Elder Lady chapel), Durham (Chapel of the Nine Altars), Ely (quire and transepts), Lincoln (nave and chapter house), Rochester (quire and transepts), Wells (nave and west front), and Worcester (quire).

Salisbury Cathedral (excluding the tower and spire) is in the Early English style and Lancet windows are used throughout, with less detailed tracery than would be used in later buildings. At Elgin, nothing substantial has survived of the nave apart from a pair of lancet windows that formerly lit one of the south aisle chapels. At Ripon more rebuilding was carried out in the 13th century under the supervision of Archbishop Walter de Grey who created the magnificent Early English west front with its series of lancet windows and sturdy twin towers. At Portsmouth the transepts retain some Norman features, such as lancet windows and arched recesses, with the later northern transept containing the slightly later cusped windows and arch. At York Minster in the north transept is the famous Five Sisters Window, each lancet being over 16 metres (52 ft) high. (see page 125)

LANTERN, in an architectural context, is a turret or other small structure that is erected on the top of a tower, roof or dome to give light to the interior of the building, as at St. Paul's, London and at Ely. When Ely's Romanesque crossing tower collapsed in 1322, there was just open space where the tower on its four great piers had been. Rather than replace the tower as it was, an enormous octagonal lantern was built over the open space.

The lantern is supported on eight large stone piers formed out of the first pairs of piers of the nave, transepts, and rebuilt choir. Above this, the superstructure is made of timber, although it was carved and painted to look like stone. Now the Ely Octagon, it is one of the most spectacular spaces ever built in an English church.

The very distinctive form of Ely Cathedral with its 'Octagon'

The interior of the Crossing and Octagon.

LAPIDARY is concerned with stones, perhaps engraved on stone, thus 'lapidarium'. We usually know this as the cutting of gems or minerals for use in the home as with Agate. At St. David's Cathedral in Wales, there is a 'lapidarium' with a display of religious stones. See also mosaic.

LECTERN is a reading desk often in the shape of an eagle, usually of brass, used to hold the Bible. In medieval times visitors were persuaded to leave money in the beak and this safeguarded the offerings from theft. In folklore, eagles are said also to be able to fly highest in the sky, so that they take the petitions of the people heavenwards, and can also fly the longest distance without a rest, so encouraging steadfastness. Newcastle, Peterborough, Southwell, Wells and York have ancient lecterns; at St. Paul's London is one made in 1720 by a Jacob Sutton for £241.

LIBRARY: most cathedrals have a library; some are very historic as cathedrals have always been a source of learning. Generally it is not possible to visit a library except by appointment as they tend to house valuable documents. However the most famous is probably Hereford which is open to visitors with its famous Chained Library and its 13th century *Mappa Mundi*, the cathedral's greatest treasure, now housed in a specially constructed building.

Salisbury and Lincoln house a copy of the Magna Carta; Canterbury, Chelmsford, Lichfield (with its Gospels of St. Chad), Manchester, Rochester and St. Paul's London have distinctive libraries with archives. Exeter has the 'Exeter Domesday', an early 1086 version of William the Conqueror's survey, and the 'Exeter Book' – that contains Anglo-Saxon poems and riddles, presented in 1050 by Edward the Confessor to the first Bishop of Exeter, Leofric. At St. David's in Wales, the library has a leaf from a manuscript of Exodus from the Welsh Bible of 1620.

LITURGY & LITURGICAL COLOURS: the liturgy (from the Greek, meaning 'work of the people') is the name in English given to:

a)   prescribed forms of public worship, specifically the Eucharist, and

b)   the texts used in public worship.

The consecration of a cathedral is an important, immense and rare event when the service and its liturgy has to be creative and appropriate: not surprisingly, the Book of Common Prayer in the Church of England does not provide such a form of service, so that when Liverpool Cathedral was to be consecrated in 1924, it was the first since that of Salisbury in 1225.

(The cathedral had an architect of genius in Giles Gilbert Scott: they found a priest, the Reverend Frederick William Dwelly, to produce the ceremonial service with proper use of the then partly completed building: he was even given the title of *Ceremoniarius*. It is said that Scott created the *body of the building*: Dwelly *brought it to life*, and for the next 30 years he was the poet and choreographer of worship in the cathedral).

Liturgical colours are also a strength in defining church seasons and events. Colours, especially on altar frontals and vestments, are used to denote the seasons and festivals of the Church, for example:

Purple, or sometimes dark blue, at Advent (for the season of preparation before Christmas), for Lent (the 40 day penitential season of preparation before Easter) and sometimes for funerals.

White at Christmas, Easter and Ascension, for feasts of the Blessed Virgin Mary and for saints who were not martyred: some cathedrals and churches now use white for funerals;

Red for Pentecost (Whitsun, Good Friday and for saints who were martyrs): Pentecost Sunday used to be named White Sunday because of the clothing worn by those who were being confirmed.

Green is the colour of creation and used throughout the season after Pentecost, normally until Advent.

Gold and white are often used for weddings.

It is often said in psychological terms that human character is in four colours: red for people who are driven; green for planners; yellow for innovators, and blue for those who care about relationships. How does this match with liturgical colours?

SEVENTEEN

MANUSCRIPT is a recording of information, manually created by someone or some people, such as a hand-written letter, as opposed to being printed or reproduced in another form. The term may also be used for information that is hand-recorded in other ways than writing, for example inscriptions that are chiselled upon a hard material or scratched (the original meaning of *graffiti*) as with a knife point in plaster or with a stylus on a waxed tablet (the way Romans made notes).The word is derived from the Latin *manu scriptum*, literally 'written by hand'. Originally, all books were in manuscript form. In China, woodblock printing was used for books from about the 7th century. In the Islamic world and the West, all books were in manuscript until the introduction of movable type printing in about 1450. Manuscript copying of books continued for a least a century, as printing remained expensive. Private or government documents remained hand-written until the invention of the typewriter in the late 19th century. The traditional abbreviations are MS for manuscript and MSS for manuscripts.

A Book of Hours contains essentially the office of the Blessed Virgin Mary, the prayers, psalms and readings for private devotional use. Famous is the *'Cardinal Stuart's Book of Hours'*. Apparently, it is the most common type of surviving medieval illuminated manuscript, and each is unique in one way or another.

A choirbook is a large-format manuscript used by choirs in cathedrals during the Middle Ages and large enough for the entire choir to read from one book! Choirbooks were generally put on a stand with smaller boy sopranos in front and the men at the rear. Many of the choirbooks were stark and utilitarian and show signs of heavy and constant use; at larger cathedrals the choirbooks were sometimes lavishly decorated and illuminated. They represented a major investment and were rarely owned by single people, but rather by families or institutions. Once the printing of music became easier and more commonplace, choirbooks were replaced by smaller, cheaper and easier to handle books.

(see 'Choirbook' for *'Choirbook for the Queen'*.)

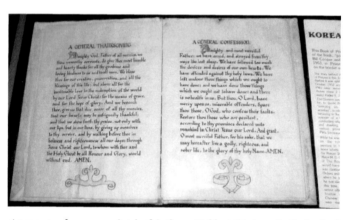

An unusual manuscript is this from Belfast St. Anne's Cathedral (located in its military chapel of remembrance) of a book of prayers that was written on rice-paper, by a prisoner of war in Korea in the 2nd World War.

The Pepys Manuscript is a late 15th century English choirbook that received its name because it was part of the collection owned by Samuel Pepys, who had described it as containing *"monkish music of the time of Edward IV"*. But it appears on evidence to have been begun a year or two earlier. (See also Book of Hours and choirbook.)

MASON and MASTER MASON: the mason is a person who builds with stone and an important person in the building of a cathedral, hence a mason's mark: a device carved on stone by the mason who dressed it. A marvellous example of an apprentice column is to be found at the Rosslyn Chapel near Edinburgh, with its fame now attached to the 'Da Vinci Code'. Masonry is a mason's work. The term 'dressing' in masonry or walls means the blocks of stone that have been 'dressed' by being worked cleverly to a smooth face and used at the corners or angles (quoins) or in a doorway and window as a frame. (The term 'freemason' also derives from 'build or strengthen with masonry'). It is interesting that some cathedrals now have their own works department with a mason or even master mason, and apprentices, to ensure future standards of work, as at St. Mary's Episcopal Cathedral in Edinburgh, and at Canterbury and Gloucester.

The master mason may be described as a combination of architect, surveyor and clerk of works who supervised the building of the cathedral. The guide book of a cathedral will usually draw attention to a master mason, if known, responsible for work at the cathedral. For example at Exeter it was Master Roger, mentioned in the Fabric Roll of 1297, and then there was Thomas of Witney, master mason from 1316 – 1242 and known as 'architect': masons left their marks here in the vault. At the building of Liverpool Cathedral, 'banker masons' are noted: apparently working in the background to prepare the stone and brick and who put their own personal mark on each stone with a code number to indicate where the stone was to be placed in the final design.

MASS: the dictionary meaning of mass is 'a coherent body of matter of indefinite shape' which some may feel is rather like a setting of the Mass, a celebration of the Eucharist in the Roman Catholic or Anglican/Episcopal Churches of the Catholic tradition. That known as 'High Mass' is with music, three ministers at the altar (priest, deacon and subdeacon) and usually with incense. 'Low Mass' has no music and the minimum of ceremony.

MEMORIALS are by statue, building, festival or religious service: serving to commemorate, in the form of a chantry, monument, shrine, statue, tablet or tomb, as described under these headings. Bath Abbey is said to have the largest number of memorials other than Westminster Abbey, and is noteworthy for the number of Scots who are remembered for army service and trade, and perhaps were in Bath for the 'waters'. Gloucester Cathedral houses over 400 memorials and monuments. The east end of York Minster is crammed with memorials. Some are painted Elizabethan and Jacobean depicting husbands, wives and children dressed in fine clothes.

An unusual modern memorial at Carlisle is that of a policeman's face sculpted in stone, with spectacles and helmet, high on the exterior wall of the cathedral, in recognition of a policeman killed in service.

St. Magnus Cathedral of Orkney has its unique 17th century memorials of grave-markers now located in each aisle – reminders of life and death (see under aisle). It also has a memorial as a harsh reminder of when the 'Royal Oak' was sunk by a German U-boat in 1939, which is dedicated to the memory of the hundreds of sailors who died. Now, once a week, a single page of the memorial book is turned as a reminder of the loss of life.

MESSIAH has many meanings but is basically a deliverer or liberator of oppressed people. In the Jewish religion he is the promised deliverer of and for the Jews. In Christian terms Jesus Christ is The Messiah. It is a term that has probably caused more argument and anxiety than any other and cannot be defined more adequately here. Many books and websites give contrasting views and it is advisable to read and compare, especially what is at the essence of the Christian faith.

Messiah is also an English oratorio, perhaps the most famous composed by George Frideric Handel, and considered to be one of the greatest works in the history of music and certainly one of the most popular in western choral works. The libretto by Charles Jennens is drawn entirely from the King James and Great Bibles, and interprets the Christian doctrine of the Messiah. Handel deliberately called his oratorio 'Messiah', but it is often incorrectly called The Messiah.

MINSTER: See under earlier entry.

MINISTER is a term used mainly in politics, as the head of a government department – in Scotland as the 'First Minister' and for the United Kingdom as the 'Prime Minister'. It has probably been made more popular due to the BBC programme and stage-play *Yes Minister.*

A minister of religion is described as a religious worker whose main duty is to lead a congregation in prayer and preach about their religious beliefs.

There are a range of references to leadership in the New Testament. In Colossians 1:25, "I became its servant according to God's commission that was given to me for you, to make the word of God fully known…" One of the clearest references is found in 1 Timothy 3:1-16, which outlines the requirements of a minister or bishop (interpreted as elder by some denominations): "The saying is sure: whoever aspires to the office of bishop desires a noble task. Now a bishop must be above reproach," etc. (New Revised Standard Version of the Bible).

MISERICORD is a hinged seat, in the choir stalls of a medieval church, which when tipped up gives support to a person standing during a lengthy service, as used by monks in medieval times, and perhaps more recently! (Possibly from the old French meaning of 'compassionate' or from Latin of 'mercy'.) Because of their relative obscurity under the seats, misericords probably suffered less destruction than most of the other furniture during the Reformation and Civil War, and this gives them a rather special role as records of the art and interests of common folk 'written' by themselves. The cathedral misericords are usually humorously or grotesquely carved and interesting.

Chester has 48 misericords dating from 1390 (one depicted here) and five more modern ones, perhaps the finest in Britain.

Beverley Minster has 68 misericord seats, carved in 1520, believed to be the largest collection in the world, and possibly the work of the Ripon Carvers, with the largest collection of musicians playing medieval instruments.

Winchester's date from 1308; Chichester's date from the 14th century, and look for 'the longest kiss in history'.

Ely has 14th century attractive misericords; Gloucester also 14th century with a wooden effigy of the Duke Robert, the eldest son of William the Conqueror, between the stalls; Norwich's are 15th century; St. Paul's London are 17th century, and Durham offers later examples from the 17th century.

A search in all the cathedral quires for these carvings and for the coats of arms and the canopies is fascinating and rewarding. It is often disappointing that in many cathedrals the seats, when not in use, are generally left down (for safety and care) so that the misericords cannot be seen. Always seek permission to view or photograph. There is an outstanding website for all cathedrals: www.misericords.co.uk

A 'misericord' is the description also of an apartment in a monastery in which relaxation of rules was permitted and also a dagger for giving the 'coup de grace' – an interesting link, perhaps!

See also entry under choir or quire for more details.

MITRE is an archbishop's, bishop's and abbot's tall cap, triangular in shape, deeply cleft at the top and worn as a symbol of office. An example at a particular cathedral is often on display in its treasury.

MONK & MONASTERY: a monastery is the residence of a community usually of monks, and similarly of nuns, living secluded under religious vows: thus a monastic order of monks or nuns in a monastery. In England there were about 650 monasteries when Henry VIII dissolved them in 1536-1539 and comprised mainly Benedictines, Cistercians, Augustinians and Carthusians. Many monasteries were then demolished, but several became cathedrals after the Dissolution.

Bangor Cathedral was previously a Monastery of 525, rebuilt 1120 – 1139, and then destroyed on more than one occasion and subsequently extensively rebuilt by Sir Gilbert Scott from 1868. It has a biblical garden with every plant mentioned in the Bible.

An attractive website of a 'Cathedral Cave' at the National Showcase Centres for Wales near Brecon is: www.showcaves. co.uk

MONUMENTS: seen by the score on the walls of nearly all cathedrals to men and women who have played a significant part in the history and achievements of the cathedral and abbey, and possibly the city or district. They provide an insight into trade and professions and to a past source of income for the cathedral, and make for fascinating reading.

Some are highly ornate as in this at the Armagh RC Cathedral.

In Canterbury Cathedral there is a notable monument to Edward the Black Prince.

St. Paul's London has, probably, the most famous found above the tomb of its architect, Sir Christopher Wren, in a quiet corner of the crypt. Part of the text *"SI MONUMENTUM REQUIRIS CIRCUMSPICE"* is loosely translated as *"If you seek his monument, look around you"*.

That, surely, is a message for all in a cathedral!

MOSAIC is the art of creating images with an assemblage of small pieces of coloured glass, stone (as in lapidary) or other material. It may be a technique of decorative art, an aspect of interior decoration, or of cultural and spiritual significance as in a cathedral.

Probably the finest mosaic in Britain is a pavement, the Cosmati pavement, before the high altar in Westminster Abbey – a mosaic floor of over 50,000 pieces of marble, stone, glass and metal from 1268, and then the centrepiece of the abbey during its rebuilding by Henry III. It is the best surviving example, outside of Italy, of this type of mosaic known as 'Cosmati' and named after a Roman family of marble workers. Amazingly with foresight, the then Abbot of Westminster, Richard de Ware, had witnessed similar work in Anagni Cathedral in Italy in 1260 and decided to commission the pavement.(He is buried under the north side of the pavement). It is intricate, complex and beautiful, one of the greatest of medieval treasures and hidden from view since the 1870s, but now being diligently conserved so that it may be displayed. Visit when completed not only to view its beauty but to marvel at its history for the central orb in this pavement is the place where kings and queens have been crowned for centuries, including our present Queen Elizabeth. Revel in its history and beauty and then look up and around to view other mysteries in this royal peculiar.

There is also the unusual TESSELLATED PAVEMENT, mentioned here because the finest example is in the Roman Catholic Westminster Cathedral in London. It is a floor covered with small blocks of mosaic consisting of marble and other material; and this cathedral has also very fine chapels with rich mosaics.

This mosaic roof of the baptistery at St. Anne, Belfast, is a magnificent example of art adapted to the Romanesque style of architecture with its emphasis on space, on the walls and domed roof.

The roof itself is composed of 150,000 pieces of glass representing creation and symbolising earth, fire and water.

MOULDINGS are important ornamental lines of grooving or channels that are worked above or below a plain surface, often enriched with carved foliage or other forms. Importantly, mouldings varied in successive historical periods of architecture so that experts can tell often the date of the building from the moulding.

MULLION is a stone or wood vertical bar dividing a window-opening into lights.

EIGHTEEN

NARTHEX is a railed-off western porch. At the RC Cathedral of St. John the Baptist in Norwich, there is a new narthex as a place to look and learn, to visit and find out about the history of the cathedral. The £2m project will improve physical and intellectual access to this Grade 1 listed cathedral, the second largest RC cathedral in Britain from 1910 designed by George Gilbert Scott Jr., and probably the most complete example of Neo-Gothic ecclesiastical architecture in the country.

NAVE is the main part of a church, with or without aisles, but excluding the chancel and transepts (if any) – and where the public was allowed when the building was monastic. In front of the pulpitum (the screen dividing nave from choir) was the altar at which the Eucharist was celebrated, and often still is in many cathedrals and churches. One can still see seating, around the wall of the nave and usually of stone in recesses, that was available for the elderly or infirm or those feeling unwell, that apparently provoked the saying, *"the weakest to the wall"*.

Durham's nave is astounding; the slender piers alternate with massive drum columns.

The naves at the larger cathedrals, for example at Durham, Gloucester, Liverpool and York, are best viewed and experienced without its seating, when not in use for a service or event, to give a feeling of immense size and space.

The nave at York Minster, empty of chairs
(by courtesy of BBC North Yorkshire)

The nave of York Minster is emptied of its furniture once a year, at a quiet time in the minster's year, to see the nave free of its 800 chairs. The building of the Nave began in 1280, and took 70 years to complete. When work commenced the builders were worried by the weight of the stone vaulting and spanned the space with wood, creating one of the purest and most beautiful architectural features of any building in Britain. Built in the Decorated style, it replaced the old Norman Nave of Thomas of Bayeux, as the widest Gothic nave in England. On entering the cathedral through the west door one is immediately impressed by the sheer scale of the surroundings and a statue on the right shows the minster's patron saint, St. Peter, holding his symbol, a key.

Different uses of the nave are not a modern innovation; in medieval times, the nave would have been used for a variety of purposes: markets were held there, and in the 1500s there were complaints about boys playing football in the nave!

St. Albans, shown here, is said to have the longest nave in England of 85 metres (275 ft 6 ins) that displays the Romanesque arches of the 11th century, Early English arches from the early 13th century enlargement, and decorated arches from a rebuilding after a partial collapse in 1323.

Fine naves can also be experienced at Ely, (the nave was built in the early 12th century, so the architectural style is Romanesque, originally with 13 bays when such long naves were typical of Anglo-Norman cathedrals and monasteries) and at Chichester, Edinburgh Episcopal, Exeter, Hereford, Lincoln, Peterborough and Southwell.

Newcastle is unusual in that the nave is more narrow than the side aisles which had 18 chantry chapels in earlier times. Belfast St. Anne's has a nave with ten pillars that are topped by carvings depicting Belfast life.

At Canterbury a major archaeological discovery has revealed an Anglo-Saxon cathedral (probably burnt down in 1067 and almost as big as its successor) under the flagstones of the nave of the cathedral.

NEEDLEWORK is part and parcel of embroidery. The Royal School of Needlework is the international centre for embroidery teaching based at Hampton Court Palace in south-west London. The National Needlework Archive in London maintains a documentary and photographic record of textiles located in the community throughout the United Kingdom. The quality of needlework and embroidery in cathedrals is superb; some ancient if not damaged by war and fire, some from professional designers and makers, but much from volunteers. Most cathedrals have a needlework group working on old and new. Rare and exquisite fragments of Anglo-Saxon needlework from Worcester, nearly 1,000 years old, are currently being restored: they are the only surviving pieces from the same period as the famous Bayeux Tapestry in France and are among the very earliest examples of English embroidery.

(It is possible that they may have been part of vestments which belonged to St. Wulfstan, Bishop of Worcester from 1062 until 1095, whose 1,000th anniversary of his birth was celebrated in 2008. The fragments were discovered in a stone coffin in 1870 during building work in the Lady chapel of the cathedral and are thought to have been concealed there by monks who venerated St. Wulfstan and feared the embroidery pieces might be destroyed at the time of the Reformation. They had been stored until recently in a drawer in the library).

NINETEEN

ORGAN: the most powerful of instruments. Philanthropist Andrew Carnegie, who had an organ in his Scottish home at Skibo Castle, once said that *"the Organ took him nearer to God"*. It has its origins in the 3rd century, and by the 8th century had been introduced into Christian worship. Winchester in the 10th century had an organ with over 400 pipes and 26 bellows – it is not known how many men were required to pump the bellows! Records at Worcester state that in the 14th century payments were made to a musician *"to thump the organs, teach quire boys, and to instruct any of the monks who wished to learn the art of organ thumping"*.

Durham had an organ in the 13th century. Many organs were removed as 'superstitious' by order of Queen Elizabeth in 1563, coming again into use late in the 17th century.

The organ case in fine wood, often decorated, is a most attractive and prominent feature with its pipe-work, some gilded and some in silver, and often in different sections even with special pipe effects in a distant balcony, visible to the visitor.

The main organ is occasionally located above the screen separating nave from chancel, and one sometimes wonders how the organist can accompany the choir: the use of mirrors is a special accomplishment. Apparently Sir Christopher Wren was keen on organs in his London churches, although by 1708 only 12 had been installed in 50 of the churches. He favoured the placing in a western gallery.

Derby has its 1939 Compton organ and Sebastian Comper 1963 case in the gallery over the doors leading into the nave, with its 3,077 pipes, some from preceding instruments of 1808 and 1879.

Unless by appointment for a special purpose, the organ and organ-lofts are not accessible for a visit. Each cathedral takes great pride in its organ, and in its choir, and the regular organ recitals and concerts are features to be experienced.

'Father' Henry Willis is a name that occurs regularly as an organ builder, one of the most prolific of the 19th century with his work seen at Canterbury, Edinburgh Episcopal, Gloucester, Hereford, Lincoln, Salisbury, Truro and Winchester, and St. Paul's London.

The grand organ at the Westminster RC Cathedral is considered to be the greatest achievement of Henry Willis III, but Liverpool Anglican must also rank as a great achievement. At the consecration service in 1924 only part of the organ was complete (along with only part of the cathedral!) but the dedication service in 1926 provided a unique occasion when some words of Milton were sung:

"Ring out, ye crystal spheres,
Once bless our human ears;
And let the bass of Heaven's deep organ blow
And, with your nine-fold harmony,
Make up full concert to the angelic symphony".

See the poem also under 'chapel'.

There are fine new organs in Edinburgh – at St. Giles' Cathedral. The new 1992 organ retained the Pedal Open Wood 16' and the Bombarde 32' from the previous Willis III 1940 instrument. There are 57 speaking stops and the louvred top of the central pipe tower contains a ring of 37 Whitechapel bells, which are playable from the Swell manual and from the Pedal.

At the St. Mary's Metropolitan (RC) Cathedral, the organ has 63 speaking stops and two consoles, one in the west gallery as shown here with the pipes, and one movable in the chancel where for recitals the organist is visible to the audience.

St. Anne Belfast has the largest pipe organ in Northern Ireland, as here in the choir stalls, that is beautifully designed from 1907, and was rebuilt in 1969 and 1975.

Visit to view fine Organ Cases from the:

17th C: Bristol; Durham; Gloucester; Newcastle; Christ Church, Oxford; St. Paul's London.

18th C: Wakefield.

19th C: Chichester; Ely; Lincoln; Portsmouth;

Ripon; Rochester, Winchester; York;

and in Wales: Bangor and St. Asaph.

20th C: Bradford; Chelmsford; Lichfield; Guildford; Liverpool; Peterborough; St. Albans and Derby.

If a reader has a particular interest in cathedral organs, choirs and music it is possible to learn more and support the cathedral music by subscribing to *Friends of Cathedral Music* with its excellent twice-yearly publication: Friends of Cathedral Music; 27 Old Gloucester Street, London WC1N 3AX. Tel: 0845 6443721. Email: info@fcm.org.uk Web: www.fcm.org.uk

ORIENTATION: not a description of one's religion, but the compass alignment of a church where the altar is usually orientated to the east. Most cathedrals in Britain are orientated west to east with the nave commencing at the west, and with quire and chancel with altar at the east.

Salisbury is one of 20 cathedrals built after the Battle of Hastings in 1066 when William the Conqueror seized control of England and Wales: built in the Early English Gothic style it has a simple lay-out in the shape of a cross with west to east orientation and two transepts providing the 'wings' (as shown here). However, the floorplan of each cathedral is different, often with added chapels and chapter house, and the printed guide always provides the plan of the cathedral.

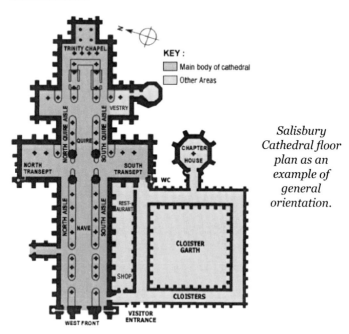

Salisbury Cathedral floor plan as an example of general orientation.

TWENTY

PAINTINGS: walls of cathedrals and churches were painted in medieval times. Along with stained glass, these paintings provided the visual story especially for those unable to read, and as a record of events and to make the building colourful. Some became known as the 'Poor Man's Bible'. Evidence of early painting can still be witnessed in some cathedrals and churches. At St. Albans in the nave and elsewhere there is a series of outstanding 13th and 14th century wall paintings, hidden after the Reformation and rediscovered in the 19th century.

More recently several cathedrals have commissioned fine art for display on the walls with paintings, tapestries and sculptures. At Chichester there is Graham Sutherland's 'Mary Magdalene meets Christ in the Garden;' in St. Paul's London there is Holman Hunt's *'Light of the World'*; in St. Mary's Episcopal of Edinburgh there are fine examples of the religious work of the artist Sir Robin Philipson, one of the major figures of 20th century Scottish painting; and of course, in Coventry Cathedral is the famous Sutherland masterpiece in tapestry *'Christ in Glory'* complemented by John Piper/ Patrick Reyntiens' baptistry window.

PARAPET is the low wall built around a roof or platform to prevent people from falling over the edge and observed at the top of a cathedral if ascending the tower – beware!

PEW is a wooden seat or bench in the church. Pews only appeared at the end of the medieval period and a congregation almost never had pews or chapel chairs until the Reformation. Quire pews face inwards to assist antiphonal chanting (sung alternately by the choir each side). At Christ Church Oxford, the quire seems to fill the nave up to the chancel.

The term 'bench-end' describes the end of a bench or seat from the late Gothic period, often carved with foliage, heraldry and sometimes grotesque human or animal shapes.

From the 1600s through the mid 1800s, churchgoers of most denominations were seated in their houses of worship according to social rank, whether by assignment or purchase. The highest ranking pews were close to the pulpit, the lowest furthest from the pulpit. To the outsider the effect of renting pews in any church was off-putting and wrong, and caused much debate. It is not certain when the practice ended but it certainly declined in the 19th century due to work of reformers and ended with the trend to remove pews. Older churches in general in their history describe frankly the changes and some tell wonderful stories, such as at a church in Carmarthenshire where *"Mrs Crawshaw brought her dogs and had tea served on a table in her pew during service"*. For an interesting and challenging background about the development of pews, see the website www.churchantiques. com/pews

The Anglican Cathedral in Sheffield, as with Ripon (see under chairs), is considering replacement with chairs, but intending to save its bench-ends. Contrarily, Leeds Roman

Catholic Cathedral – during a restoration – has installed new modern pews in light wood that blend well with the fabric of the building.

PILASTER is a slightly projecting column built into or applied to the face of a wall; usually flattened or rectangular in form, it can also take a half-round form or the shape of any type of column. In classical architecture it is used to give the appearance of a supporting column with only an ornamental function. Pilasters may appear on the sides of a door frame or window opening on the facade of a building. As with a column, a pilaster can have a plain or fluted surface to its profile and can be represented in any architectural style. The fashion of using this element from Ancient Greek and Roman architecture was adopted in the Italian Renaissance, gained wide popularity with Greek Revival architecture, and continues to be seen in modern architecture. The modern Brentwood RC Cathedral in Essex is famous for its four giant Doric pilasters in the Italian Renaissance style.

PILGRIM is a person who journeys to a sacred place as an act of religious devotion, a traveller, and as in *Pilgrim's Progress 'one journeying to a future life'*. Initially a main destination was the Holy Land, still popular today, to places such as Jerusalem associated with Jesus, his mother Mary and disciples. When the Roman Empire collapsed many places were closed off, but then pilgrimages were revived especially with the Crusades of the 12th and 13th centuries. It is interesting for a modern religious and 'artistic' link that St. Francis of Assisi created 'Stations of the Cross' as a form of devotion and where, now, images by paintings or sculpture on the walls of cathedrals and churches, display the sequence of the passion, death and resurrection of Jesus. One can walk the Stations of the Cross through the now crowded shopping alleys of Jerusalem, and many walk 'The Way of the Cross' in their own cathedrals and churches especially in Holy Week during the season of Lent each year.

Pilgrimages also occurred to the shrines of famous saints especially in cathedrals: two of the greatest are the shrine of St. Thomas Becket in Canterbury Cathedral and also at the Shrine of our Lady in Little Walsingham in Norfolk. Hereford is also important as it has three 'kinds' of saint: St. Ethelbert – a saint of pre-medieval times; St. Thomas – a medieval saint (offerings at his shrine helped rebuild the central tower with its ball-flower decoration); and Thomas Traherne from 1674, known as a Church of England 'holy person'.

Shrines could attract numerous pilgrims, sometimes of great wealth that assisted the religious order and building. Badges were sold for pilgrims to collect, also as proof of participation. Cathedrals with important shrines for pilgrimage are: Canterbury, Chester, Chichester, Durham, Ely, Lincoln, Oxford, Rochester, St. Alban's, and Winchester (the last resting place of St. Swithun from the 9th century).

PORCH is a covered approach to the entrance to a building; sometimes termed a 'draught excluder', later developed perhaps with a room above for meetings or even lodgings for the clergy. Nowadays a main entrance for visitors is often not that initially built as the entrance, so one has to enquire if interested in the porch or look for the main west entrance to see what is housed there. There are 'Galilee' porches where the Palm Sunday Gospel is, or was, read from the porch, possibly at Chichester, Durham and Ely, where the custom was for the bishop, after the reading, to knock on the door with his crosier (his crook/pastoral staff) asking for entrance, and thus 'the entry into Jerusalem' (see also under sanctuary).

PRESBYTERY is the eastern part of a chancel beyond the choir – the area near the high altar and a sanctuary. At St. Albans the presbytery has a unique 13th century wooden vaulted ceiling, which was redecorated in the 15th century. (Presbytery is often used in the Roman Catholic Church as the title of a parochial clergy house.)

PRIOR's DOOR: The prior was an officer in a monastic order or religious house, sometimes next in rank below an abbot, so doorways were named after the prior for his use. At Ely there is the magnificent and rare surviving example of the door that used to lead into the cloisters, with 12th century Romanesque carvings that date from about 1150; its tympanum depicts Christ in majesty held aloft by archangels and blessing the creatures of the universe. Two human heads peer down from the corners and the sides have medallions populated by various beasts and humans, and (as shown) with 'a drinking man'.

That at Norwich has an elaborately moulded arch, beautifully detailed in colour and displaying a splendid array of sculptures.

PSALMS: The word is derived from the Greek 'psalmoi', meaning *'songs sung to a harp'*, from 'psallein' to play on a stringed instrument, and thence from Hebrew of 'praise' as a book of the Hebrew Bible. Together, the 150 sacred poems express virtually the full range of Israel's faith.

New Testament references show that the earliest Christians, following Jewish tradition, used the psalms in worship and they have remained an important part of worship in most Christian Churches. St. Benedict, in the early 6th century, explained in his Holy Rule how his monks were to daily pray the psalms and Benedictine monks have continued this practice to the present day. Many lay people make the psalms a part of their daily prayers. The psalms and canticles (other songs from the Bible), and accompanying prayers change according to the season and the day. The psalm is a key part of the Liturgy of Matins and Evensong and the Book of Psalms still consists of 150 psalms, each of which constitutes a religious song, though one or two are lengthy and may constitute a set of related chants.

Psalm 23, *'The Lord is My Shepherd'*, is possibly the best-known and offers an appealing message of comfort, widely used in church funeral services, either as a reading or in one of several popular hymn settings.

PSALTER is a volume of the Book of Psalms that often contains other devotional material. In the early Middle Ages Psalters were amongst the most popular types of illuminated manuscripts, rivalled only by the gospel books, from which they gradually took over as the type of manuscript chosen for lavish illumination. Medieval Psalters often included a calendar, a litany of saints, canticles from the Old and New Testaments, as well as other devotional texts. The Psalter may also have been part of the breviary, and the later Book of Hours, used to say the Liturgy of the Hours in the Eastern and Western Christian worlds. (See also Book of Hours, hymns and manuscripts).

PULPIT is the raised enclosed platform, with steps or stair, and usually with a small desk from which the preacher delivers the sermon, and is normally made of wood or stone, but occasionally of marble. Some have a canopy or overhang, as shown at Salisbury Cathedral, said to protect the priest from something or someone, but probably to ensure speech was projected forward and not upwards – before the days of amplification! All cathedrals have at least one pulpit, usually in the nave and possibly one in the quire area.

Occasionally, there appear to be two rather similar in the nave, although one is the lectern.

Pulpits from the 15th century are at Norwich and Winchester; 16th century Carlisle; 17th century Portsmouth and Wells; 18th century Lincoln; 20th century York and St. Paul's London.

PULPITIM is a stone 'screen' that stretches across the cathedral and divides the nave from the quire area. Most people would call this the screen, but the more modern screen, usually of wood, is not a pulpitum that had doorways either side to provide for processions. The pulpitum was often richly decorated with coloured statues and only a few remain, as at Canterbury, Ripon, Rochester and York, and at Lincoln the pulpitum screen between the nave and St. Hugh's choir, and covered in fine stone carvings, is described by Pevsner as "a gorgeous piece of 1330s decoration": it still has traces of the original red, blue and gold colouring.

That at St. Patrick's in Down, Northern Ireland, is a striking feature topped by the organ whose pipes reach almost to the vaulted roof.

TWENTY-ONE

QUIRE (see also choir): The quire is at the east end; at St. Paul's London it was the first part of the cathedral to be built and consecrated: the quire stalls here feature delicate carvings by Grinling Gibbons, whose work is seen in many great houses.

The quire at Durham (above) is said to 'have everything'!

REFECTORY, still used to describe some cathedral cafes, was a dining-room in a monastery and existing in former monastic cathedrals, as at Chester.

REFORMATION: At the Reformation in England and Wales – the time of the Dissolution of the monasteries 1536

– 1553 in Henry VIII's reign – there was great destruction and loss of medieval church treasures. At Chichester, brasses were removed from memorials and many stone figures and carvings defaced: the shrine of St. Richard was totally destroyed with its medieval stained glass. Further damage to the cathedral and its contents, notably the library, took place at the hands of parliamentary troops when they took possession of the city at the end of 1642. At Peterborough, St. Oswald's Arm (the then abbey's most valued relic) disappeared from its chapel at the time of the reformation but the chapel still has its watch-tower where monks kept guard over it day and night.

Brasses were victims of iconoclasm (the breaking of images) particularly during the Reformation and Cromwellian eras when cartloads of brasses were ripped up and melted down.

Behind their high altar, Winchester, Southwark and St. Albans (as here) have large stone screens from the early 16th century.

See also Appendix D.

REREDOS is from the early English and French of 'areredos' – behind or back – and is the ornamental screen covering the east wall at the back of the high altar, or free-standing behind the high altar. Originally it could have been an embroidered cloth, but often since replaced by either stone or woodwork, with the scene usually of the crucifixion of

Christ, or the Last Supper. Occasionally in a stone reredos is the inscription: '*I am the Vine*', interwoven with the branches of a vine representing 'ye are the branches'. Many reredos were destroyed at the time of the Reformation and Civil War so those saved are especially valuable and noteworthy.

The unique modern 'reredos' tapestry at Coventry was designed by Graham Sutherland and at Chichester (below) by John Piper.

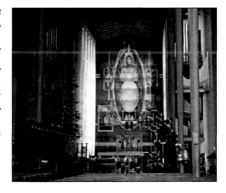

RESTORATION is important but not always without trouble, and is the replacement of damaged or worn features of an old building, or the insertion of fresh substitutes, if the item is already a replacement. Somewhat different from repairs, restoration has always caused controversy, even bitterness in Victorian times, between those who wish to replace everything as imagined to have been originally, and those who wish to modernise.

Chester is said to have suffered much from Victorian restorers, although this is not self-evident when one views, for example, the wonderful medieval woodcarvings in the choir-stalls.

(The cathedral has the most complete medieval monastic complex in the UK and records of a church on the site date back to the early 10th century. Originally built by Saxon canons in the name of the lady Saint Werburgh, the second church on the site was built by Hugh 'Lupus' (the Wolf), Earl of Chester, in 1092. Anselm of Bec, later Archbishop of Canterbury, helped found Hugh's monastic settlement at Chester. A third church was begun in 1250, this time in Norman Gothic style, built over the top of the old church, which was dismantled from the inside. The church was raised to cathedral status by Henry VIII. At the shrine to St. Werburgh one can see the niches where medieval sufferers rested their heads while spending the night in a prayer for healing).

It is believed that there are only two other cathedrals in England where the quality of the wood carving is comparable to Chester: one is Lincoln Cathedral, the other is Beverley Minster.

An example of difficulties faced was at Winchester where there has been a cathedral since about 648 AD. In its 900 years the cathedral has been greatly remodelled and extended:

The foundations of the current cathedral were laid out in 1079 by Walkelin, the first Norman bishop. To this new building (consecrated in 1093) the relics of St. Swithin were solemnly transferred, 15 July, and the old minster was torn down. The Norman cathedral measured 535 ft (164m) in length, the longest then in existence: the Norman towers at the West front were removed about 1350. Before that, there were problems. Proposed towers on the transept ends were abandoned due to poor ground conditions, and in 1107 the central tower had collapsed. In 1202 the retrochoir was begun. Between 1350-1410 the West front was rebuilt and the nave remodelled in the Perpendicular style. This was accomplished by cutting the Norman stonework in-situ and recasting the piers. The elevations were altered from the original three-storey work into two-storey by cutting out the heads of the Norman arched arcade and resetting them at a higher level. The whole nave was also re-vaulted at this time. In 1500 the east bay of the Lady chapel was rebuilt. Between 1905-12 William Walker, a diver, worked with 150 others to underpin most of the cathedral…. and so on and so on.

However, one new restoration that is very satisfactory is at Leeds RC Cathedral with reordering and restoration that focuses around the relocated sanctuary with new elements designed using a 'simple vocabulary' of stone and oak, the same materials used in the construction of the cathedral. New purpose-designed oak pews and a York stone floor add to the quality.

RETABLE: an ornamental shelf, or decorated panel, above and behind an altar, often with a ledge on which candles or crosses would be placed. Not often described or seen, there is at Norwich in its Lady chapel one dating from the 14th century.

RETROCHOIR in a cathedral and large church is the part of the chancel behind the high altar.

ROBES: the use of robes is mentioned in the Old Testament of the Bible, and linen robes have long been used in religious ceremonies, and in fact in the early church white robes used to be worn by all the congregation. Eventually, those newly baptised wore white as a sign of purity as did girls, and sometimes boys, about to be confirmed.

Today, the white robe is the surplice worn over a black, blue or red or even green cassock by choir, choirmaster and organist, and the clergy in services. In fact it used to be custom to witness clergy daily in the black cassock, but that practice is now generally abandoned in favour of the white 'dog-collar' worn under a suit – though even that practice is diminishing. The cassock is still in use as everyday dress by clergy in cathedral precincts. There are various directions in early prayer books as to when and how the surplice and hoods should be worn by the clergy, and from 1549 the surplice was *"appointed to be worn in the saying of Matins and Evensong, baptising and burying"*.

There does not appear to be a direction about the wearing of a cassock or surplice by the choir although it is reported that there is a canon of 1604 that directs students in colleges to wear the surplice at time of divine service, which may be the origin of why members of a choir wear surplice and cassock.

The biretta, a square cap of various colours, is still worn as headdress especially in the Roman Catholic Church and is a development of a 'Canterbury Cap'.

It is questionable whether robes are strictly 'vestments' but to create an overall picture they can be included and are often displayed together along with the more ceremonial vestments in the treasury of the cathedral (see also vestments).

ROOD LOFT & SCREEN: not often witnessed, the loft is a gallery across the entrance to the chancel carried on a 'rood-beam' and supporting the rood (a crucifix) and sometimes flanked by statues of saints. However, all were ordered to be demolished as superstitious in 1561 down to the 'beam', so that only modern examples are seen. The 'screen' is ornamental wooden, crowned by a crested cornice that fills the space between the underside of the beam and floor.

Chester has a magnificent rood screen separating choir from nave, with the figure of Jesus on the cross with Mary and John on either side, replacing an earlier stone screen and designed by George Gilbert Scott in 1876 that blends well with the 14th century woodwork beyond. Roods often had figures of the Virgin Mary on one side and St. John on the other.

This rood in St. Mary's Screen in St. Mary's Episcopal Cathedral, Edinburgh, is hung above the entrance to the choir and dominates the view in the aisle. It was designed by architect Sir Robert Lorimer to form part of the war memorial: Christ (whose figure was designed by Pilkington Jackson) is depicted as the suffering servant, surrounded symbolically by the four gospel writers, with the cross covered in Flanders poppies. (see page 165)

ROOF BOSS, in architectural terms, is a carved or sculptured projection at the intersecting point of ribs; dramatic and colourful in most cathedral ceilings. View each ceiling, and at the intersection of the ribs of the vaulting roof bosses are the keystone often with marvellous carvings, perhaps floral or insignia. Sometimes the cathedral provides a special moveable large mirror to view the bosses and save the strain on the neck muscles, because otherwise binoculars may be needed.

Magnificent bosses are at Canterbury, Winchester, Worcester, and as here at Norwich: and also at York, where there is a modern design following the fire of 1984, apparently from prize-winning entries from a BBC *Blue Peter* competition of over 32,000 submissions from children.

Lincoln cloisters has carved oak roof bosses with a different and difficult subject matter:

if a visitor is familiar with the themes of Christian imagery some subjects will be readily recognised, but many will still appear to be mysterious and fantastic – of the original hundred roof bosses, one in each of its bays, there are now just 60 remaining and are in five categories: religious and secular figures, heads, animals and foliage.

ROOF: as distinct from a ceiling, is the upper covering of the building that is either a timber structure of a hammer beam variety, or stone vaulting, that can start with the simple barrel vault of the 12th century up to the fan vault of the 15th century.

If the opportunity arises on a visit to a cathedral attempt the tour to the upper reaches and view the roof space to witness the structure. The guide may point out the substantial 'roof trusses' that are the framed structure of timber (timber in earlier buildings; steel and concrete in more modern), and with a 'tie beam' – a horizontal beam 'tying together' the sloping rafters to prevent them from spreading under the weight of the roof. One can see the awesome nature of the building and why it costs so much to maintain it, and also possibly view the bell chamber, and obtain a wonderful view of the surrounding countryside, as at Hereford.

The roof tour at Exeter is also exceptional for its Norman or Romanesque towers, bell tower, internal gutterings and wooden timbers – described as 'an experience of a lifetime'!

ROSE WINDOW: usually one of the glories of a cathedral: a circular window containing tracery and reminiscent of a rose. That at Westminster Abbey in its south transept, also

with the poets' corner, is the largest of its type with petal-like tracery reminiscent of later fan-vaulting.

At Lincoln, two magnificent Rose windows face one another across the north-south transept and light the great transepts. They were first made in the early 13th century and are described as 'the two eyes of the church'.

The earliest is the 'Dean's Eye' window (left) in the north transept dating from 1220, still with much of its original mediaeval glass depicting the Last Judgement. The Dean's Eye is a fine example of early English tracery: the subject of the window appears to be 'The Last Judgement' although some insertions of a different character have been introduced.

There is also a 'Teaching Window': the story of the calling of Samuel, in the lower medallion, with the centre medallion of Christ with the teachers in the temple, and the top one of Christ teaching 'Render unto Caesar' as a memorial to George Boole now regarded as one of the

The 'Bishop's Eye' window in the south transept is filled with flowing tracery from the decorated period of 1330.

founding fathers of computing and information technology, an unsung hero of the Information Revolution. After the death of George Boole in 1864, his Lincoln friends decided they would like to raise a local memorial to him, equal to that in Cork. A meeting was held at the Guildhall on 11th January 1865, chaired by Alderman Shaw, and attended by Archdeacon Larkin and other notables. A list was opened for the purpose of providing a memorial window in the cathedral, and a further memorial in the city (if funds should permit).

£139.17s was donated, but another £50 was needed; this was collected gradually and window n31 in the north aisle was inserted.

Another unsung Rose window is this at Arundel RC Cathedral where from the exterior it rests above the fine west facade, and from the inside above its fine organ.

ROTUNDA is a term usually applied to a circular domed building, or a dome: see under dome.

ROYAL PECULIARS: A royal peculiar is a church that belongs directly to the monarch and not to any diocese or province. The concept originated in Anglo-Saxon times and developed as a result of the relationship between the Norman and Plantagenet Kings and the English Church. It is believed the following are royal peculiars: St. George's Chapel, Windsor Castle (The Queen's Free Chapel of St. George in Windsor Castle)

The Chapel Royal, St. James's Palace

The Queen's Chapel, St. James's Palace

The Chapel Royal, Hampton Court

The Chapel of St. John the Evangelist in the Tower of London

The Chapel of St. Peter ad Vincula in the Tower of London

The Royal Chapel of All Saints, Windsor

The Queen's Chapel of the Savoy

The Royal Foundation of St. Katharine

The Chapel of St. Edward, King and Martyr, Cambridge

The Palace of Holyrood, Edinburgh

The Collegiate Church of St. Peter, Westminster (Westminster Abbey)

TWENTY-TWO

SACRISTY is the room for storing sacred vessels or clergy vestments, and not usually visited.

SANCTUARY is the part of the chancel between the altar rails and the east window or screen containing the high altar, and is now a place recognised as holy; indeed some believe the holiest part of the church, temple and tabernacle.

This photo shows the quire, and the altar and reredos as part of the chancel at St. Patrick's Church of Ireland Cathedral, Armagh.

Until 1624 anyone could claim sanctuary for up to 37 days in any cathedral and in some churches, especially to evade arrest as debtor or fugitive from the law. (Many cathedral closes were sanctuaries and became areas of crime – that did not please the residents). Where the church building was the sanctuary, large knockers were attached to the main door, and even by holding the knocker, when the building was closed, sanctuary could be claimed, although that action was perhaps fraught with danger. At Durham Cathedral the original knocker from the 12th century is housed in the library and a replica attached to the door on the north-west corner of the cathedral. The porch was demolished in the 18th century by James Wyatt during his rather unfortunate restoration of the building and had been used to house *"serten men dyd lie alwaises in two chambers over said north door, that any offender dyd come and knocke, straight waie they were letten in, at any houre of the nyght"*.

(Some hospitals are now, perhaps mistakenly, replacing their chapels with sanctuaries).

Sanctuary is also generally a place of protection and preservation of birds and wild animals, but at Derby there is a special story of protection: peregrine falcons first nested on the cathedral in 2006, are seen around the tower and are now webcam-watched and kept for breeding by the Derbyshire Wildlife Trust, with its Derby Cathedral Peregrine Project. Chichester Cathedral is also a nesting site for peregrine falcons that use a turret at the base of the spire. Three female and one male chick were hatched in April 2009. During the nesting season live video of the chicks is shown inside the cathedral and on the internet.

SCHOOLS (choir): teaching has always been a strong factor in Christian houses: the Benedictine Order especially has always emphasised teaching and many of its abbeys/

cathedrals had private schools, continued today with various choir schools.

Westminster Abbey Choir School is thought to be the only school in the United Kingdom exclusively for the education of boy choristers. It is located in Dean's Yard, by Westminster Abbey, and educates 30 boys currently, aged 8–13 who sing in the Choir of Westminster Abbey which takes part in state and national occasions as well as singing Evensong every day (except Wednesday) and gives concert performances around the world. The late Sir Sydney Nicholson, founder of the School of English Church Music, now the Royal School of Church Music referred to the unique heritage of boys' choirs down the ages as *"England's oldest youth movement"*.

It is said that St. Mary's Episcopal Cathedral in Edinburgh was the first cathedral in Britain to introduce girls into a cathedral choir, and now the majority of the choristers are girls; choristers usually recruited from the St. Mary's Music School.

Bury St. Edmunds and Ely have a history of a school in the 7th century with King Edward the Confessor a pupil at the latter. Cathedrals without a choir school usually recruit choristers from local state schools.

The Choir Schools Association represents 44 schools attached to cathedrals, churches and college chapels around the country where the pupils have access to first-class schooling and musical training. More than 1200 of the 21,500 boys and girls in choir schools are choristers. Some CSA schools take children from 7-13; others are junior schools with senior schools to 18. The majority are Church of

England foundations but the Roman Catholic, Scottish and Welsh Churches are all represented. Outreach programmes each year enable nearly 5,000 workshops and performances with 494 primary schools nationwide and with a total of 28,481 children involved of whom 47% are male. More than 1,200 boy and girl choristers were part of the foundation teams that visited local primary schools and hosted public concerts in cathedrals. Independent schools provide almost all the UK's cathedral and chapel choirs, many of which have world-wide reputations. They are attached to cathedrals, churches or college chapels. A child who sings well could win a free or heavily subsidised place at a choir school. Normal ages of entry, after voice trials, are 7-9; some places are available at 10. Choir schools educate 15,000 pupils, including 1,000 choristers who receive a first-class musical and academic education.

SCREEN is usually a partition of wood or stone, sometimes with decorated wrought-iron, separating without completely cutting off one part of church from another, especially to make more convenient areas for worship. Replacing the ancient pulpitum is the more modern screen from the 19th century, with influence primarily from architect Sir George Gilbert Scott, usually erected during restoration.

The screen is usually that dividing the nave from the quire and often houses aloft the organ or part of it. Several affect the view of the chancel from the nave, but are usually most attractive.

The picture shows the mid-point of Rochester Cathedral below the organ case. Here, a row of eight statues are placed in the screen as a memorial to Dean Scott (1870–87): the statues feature saints particular to Rochester.

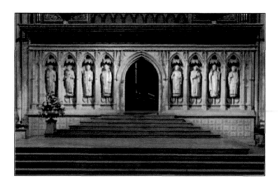

St. Mary's Glasgow, designed by Sir George Gilbert Scott (who also designed St. Mary's Episcopal Edinburgh and St. Paul's Dundee), has a wrought-iron screen designed in 1894 by John Oldrid Scott, son of Sir George.

The altar screen at Winchester has mortuary chests from 1525 balanced along the top, each marked with the name of a king and containing the bones of two bishops and five kings of Wessex. The bones are said to have become jumbled during the Civil War.

Derby has a wrought-iron screen across the whole width of the church from about 1630.

At Coventry there is a modern fine extensive screen in glass, at the west end entrance, etched with effigies of saints.

The quire screen at York was designed originally in 1420 to strengthen the tower. Part is shown here and it depicts 15 sculpted kings of England beginning with William the Conqueror, each distinct, and above is a band of angels playing

 instruments including lutes, Northumbrian pipes and sackbuts, perhaps background to the organ with its 5,000-plus pipes.

SEDILIA: a range of stone seats generally three in number – the trinity – on the south side of the chancel, for use of the clergy or servers, and usually with decorative stonework above the seating.

SERVICES: there is a regular daily pattern of worship in a cathedral usually commencing with Holy Communion at 8am, followed by Matins (or Morning Prayer) during the morning, and ending with Evening Prayer in the late afternoon or early evening. Most cathedrals now have a short period of silence at 12 noon or on the hour when visitors are asked to be stationary and quiet whilst a short prayer is pronounced. Sunday services may have different timings and the morning service will probably be a Sung Eucharist. During school term-time the Evening Service is Choral or Sung Evensong when it is usual for the congregation to sit in the quire that provides an excellent way of seeing and hearing the choir (either full choir, or lay clerks – usually men only although some women are now entering the adult choir), boys choir only or girls choir only where one is founded. Out of term-time many cathedrals have visiting choirs. It is staggering to realise the variety and amount of different hymns, anthems and service settings that members of the cathedral choir have to sing daily during the week and not all have a recognised choir school but recruit from local schools. The standard of singing and organ playing in cathedrals is of a high order and provides a wonderful experience. It is also an opportunity when sitting in the quire to reflect on the attractive and glorious woodwork and artefacts.

Visitors are welcome to participate, perhaps even when a service is 'private' for such as a memorial or thanksgiving service – always enquire. Details of services are usually available on the website of the cathedral about one week previous and always displayed at the entry or in the shop or bookstall, also normally of a high standard where profits go to the maintenance of the cathedral. The café at Chester Cathedral even houses a rich history linked to the activity of the former resident monks. That at Ely displays hand-made examples of stained glass and wall hangings; nearby is the excellent Stained Glass Museum with examples from around the world.

SHRINES are altars or chapels with special associations; a tomb of a saint and usually sculptured or highly ornamented; or simply a casket that holds sacred relics, sometimes a 'freretory'. (It can be also a Shinto place of worship, or even a place hallowed by some memory.) In the Catholic tradition it is usually a tomb formed into a small chapel that contains the relics of a saint that became a focal point of a cathedral, and is normally found behind or near to the high altar. Because shrines were objects of pilgrimages, they attracted wealth to the cathedral and to the city. The Reformation caused the destruction of many shrines, so those remaining intact are very precious and others have been restored, perhaps with some or all of the finding of the remains, and usually on the site of the original shrine.

Durham was founded in 995 as a final resting place for the remains of St. Cuthbert which had been moved around for a century since removal from Lindisfarne: Cuthbert's followers built a white church here until it was pulled down by the bishop when the present building was begun in 1093.

The shrines of St. Ethelreda at Ely, and St. Swithun at Winchester are notable.

At Christ Church Oxford especially beautiful carvings can be seen on the 13th century tomb of female St. Frideswide: made in 1289 the shrine is the cathedral's oldest monument.

At St. Albans, the shrine of St. Alban was rebuilt in the early 14th century but was destroyed at the Reformation, then rediscovered and rebuilt in the 19th century, and restored in 1993. A rare survival, it remains a centre of ecumenical worship.

A shrine in the north transept of Arundel RC Cathedral is of St. Philip Howard, whose father was beheaded by Queen Elizabeth in 1572 for plotting to marry Mary Queen of Scots; and with the current Duke of Norfolk of lineal descent. Here also is a window of royal saints including Ethelbert of Kent who founded Canterbury and also Edward the Confessor, King of England 1040-1066.

St. David's Cathedral, built in the 12th century, became one of the most important shrines of medieval Christendom – holy but not stable as its ground was swampy and even now the piers in the nave lean out a little (two pilgrimages to St. David's are said to equal one to Rome). A container made of wood and metal, kept behind the high altar, is believed to hold the bones of St. David and St. Justinian, his colleague and confessor.

The feast-day of a particular saint can usually be obtained from the website of a cathedral so that a visitor may, if so disposed, plan a visit to a shrine on that particular day.

SPIRE, STEEPLE & TOWER: three features with different definitions according to which dictionary one uses: a spire is defined as a tapering structure in the form of a tall cone or pyramid rising above the tower, or a building of considerable elevation; a steeple is a spire with bells in it, or a lofty structure especially a tower surmounted by a spire, rising above the roof of church; a tower is a building of considerable elevation or a tall, usually equilateral (esp. square) or circular structure, often part of a church, and can house machinery apparatus and operators (with the verb 'to tower' – to reach high above or over surroundings).

So there we are – one can decide what the tall structure should be called.

Salisbury has the highest spire completed in 1334 and contains medieval scaffolding and at the top a fragment of the robe of the Virgin Mary sealed in a leaden box. It is recorded that Lincoln, with its dramatic location on a high ridge overlooking the town, had in the 14th century a lead-encased spire and at 525 feet the first building to be taller than the Great Pyramid of Giza (481 feet). Until the spire fell down in 1549 it was the world's tallest building.

Oxford's is reputed to be the oldest from the 13th century.

Lichfield and Truro are two cathedrals in England with triple spires: Lichfield's west ones date from the 14th century – its central spire destroyed and rebuilt in the 17th century. Shown here, Truro has spires from the 19th century. St. Mary's Episcopal Cathedral in Edinburgh also has three spires.

St.Patrick's Newry, from 1578 and rebuilt 1866, is considered the first Protestant church in Ireland, and has an unusual spire consisting of a small steeple at each corner of the clock tower.

Unusual structures are seen at Chichester with its central 13th century tower and 19th century rebuilt spire – following many years of neglect, the restoration of the cathedral was started during the 1840s but there was a major setback to the restoration programme when the spire collapsed in 1861; the spire now is Sir George Gilbert Scott's restoration. Chichester has two architectural features that are unique among England's medieval cathedrals – a free-standing medieval bell tower (or campanile) and double aisles. The spire of Chichester Cathedral can be seen for many miles across the meadows of West Sussex and is a landmark for sailors; Chichester is thought to be the only English cathedral that is visible from the sea.

Chester has a free-standing bell tower completed 1974; Ely with a 14th century west tower and unique central 'lantern' tower rebuilt in 1322; Exeter with 12th century tower either end of transepts; Newcastle with 15th century lantern tower and with a steeple held by flying buttresses; Portsmouth with a 17th century central tower; St. Alban's with a central tower constructed with Roman tiles of Verulamium; Southwell has twin west towers with Rhenish caps; Wakefield has a 15th century 'crocketted' (with an ornament) spire; York's three towers are 15th century. At Bury St. Edmunds, its St. Edmundsbury Cathedral has a fine new millennium central tower, the only one built this century. Belfast Anglican has a new Spire of Hope, a stainless steel structure of Swiss make and design. (See also tower.)

STAFF: Visitors may see or meet clergy whilst in a cathedral, especially during a service, or hear reference to them, so it is useful to appreciate their duties. In simple terms these are:

The dean is head of the chapter with overall responsibility for business of the cathedral. In Scotland it is usually a provost.

The precentor is usually a canon with responsibility for the music, traditionally ensuring 'that the note is pitched correctly', working with the director of music or organist.

The treasurer is the keeper of the cathedral treasures. Apparently in earlier days he had to pay for the repair of any damage to them out of his own pocket; to counter this his salary was larger than his colleagues – that must have caused some problems! This is still a key post.

The prebendary in the Church of England is possibly the most unusual title and originates from 'prebend' – a piece of land, income from which paid the prebendary his salary, until 1836 when the church commissioners took over this responsibility.

A prebendary is a post connected to a cathedral or collegiate church and is a type of canon. Prebendaries had a role in the administration of the cathedral: when attending cathedral services prebendaries sat in particular seats, usually at the back of the choir stalls, known as prebendal stalls. Prebends and collegiate churches were dissolved by Henry VIII in 1547 as part of the Reformation by the Act for the Dissolution of Collegiate Churches and Chantries. However, the title prebendary was still retained by certain dioceses (with the dioceses of Lichfield and Lincoln being two examples) as an honorary title for senior parish priests. This is usually awarded as a recognition of long and dedicated service to the diocese. These priests are entitled to call themselves prebendary (usually shortened to preb.) and still have a role in the administration of the cathedral.

Canons are members of a cathedral chapter, the body responsible for the temporal and spiritual life of a cathedral. Some are appointed to specific tasks within a diocese: e.g., canon missioner, or within a cathedral: e.g., canon treasurer.

Verger, or virgir, is an official, not a member of the clergy, who undertakes certain duties and who carries a mace or wand before the clergy in procession.

Wandsmen (not a title now in regular use), or ushers, act as stewards for the services, and mainly give voluntary service. Some wear a gown, whilst in other cathedrals they may wear morning dress (most stewards and volunteers now wear a sash to distinguish them in their tasks in a cathedral, as at the welcome desk, in the shop, or as guide).

STAINED GLASS was initially an important visual aid to prayer and learning, and in fact still has that function to display a theme or story. There are varieties of stained (and painted) glass and it is worth obtaining an explanatory booklet to understand the techniques involved in their making. Generally it is glass that is stained or coloured by the addition of a metallic oxide during its burning, but usually painted afterwards with a delicate foliage or symbols. The term stained glass usually refers to the material of coloured glass or the craft of working with it: throughout its thousand-year history, the term has been applied almost exclusively to the windows of churches, cathedrals, chapels, and other significant buildings. Although traditionally made in flat panels and used as windows, the creations of modern stained glass artists also include three-dimensional structures and sculpture. The cleaning of this glass is also important and special cleaning techniques and materials are required.

Ely Cathedral has an 1857 'Tree of Jesse' window in early medieval style (based on the Book of Isaiah of the descent of the Messiah from Jesse of Bethlehem). Other cathedrals with fine ancient 'Jesse' windows include Canterbury with some richly-coloured figures from 1200; and Salisbury with 13th century glass. Wells with glass from about 1340 is also proud of this heritage.

York Minster is proud of its glass from the 12th century onwards, and surprisingly the minster did not suffer unduly during the English Civil War as the Cromwellian general, Sir Thomas Fairfax, ensured no harm came to the building. Its 'Five Sisters' window in the north transept is the oldest complete window created from the 13th century and a real contrast to the Rose window opposite (this transept is also home to the astronomical clock and often to art displays).

York Minster nave contains the West Window, constructed in 1338, with biblical scenes and figures of archbishops and apostles, and over the Lady chapel in the east end is the Great East Window, finished in 1408, and the largest expanse of medieval stained glass in the world. Look for the humour in the Zouche Chapel 15th century window with a bird seeking after a spider in its web. The south transept contains the famous Rose window. In the north transept is medieval stained glass, each lancet being over 16 metres (52 ft) high, in a 'Five Sisters' window known as 'grisaille' – a grey-green technique (of which there is a modern example in a 'Good Shepherd' window in the Church of the Good Shepherd, Murrayfield, Edinburgh).

Another interesting story is of how the making of windows does not always match the intention of the 'creators': William Wilson of Glasgow who had made some fine windows in Scotland (including at the Church of the Good Shepherd Edinburgh) was, on the strength of his work, commissioned to make the famous 'Bishop's window' at Liverpool Anglican Cathedral. The committee had not seen the finished versions in Wilson's studio and when installed the robes and face of the featured bishop and archbishop were not correct, so alterations had to be made after the window had been installed. Fortunately this took place in a bay hidden from view of the public.

Ely, of course, houses the excellent Stained Glass Museum, situated in its North Triforium Gallery, that displays fine specimens including:

a Grisaille Panel of 1220-1260 of Cistercian work; 16th century Swiss glass panels that re-awakened interest in the skills during the Gothic Revival;

from 1702 'The Last Supper' by William Price the Elder whose designed glass appears in Christ Church Oxford;

'Angel Musicians' 1860 from Derby;

Scottish glass with 'The Widow's Mite' by Daniel Cotter (1864) the pioneer of modern stained glass in Scotland;

'Queen Victoria of 1910' by Hugh Arnold who wrote 'Medieval Glass in England and France';

Irish glass of the 20th century, and more modern including the Christmas stamp of 1969 designed by David Gentleman;

and also appropriately the Arms of the Glazier Company – this worshipful company first mentioned in a list of guilds in 1328, with its arms described in 1588;

Altogether an incredible history of stained glass.

Historically, the earliest stained glass is in Canterbury Cathedral with the 12th century great west window of Adam digging in the Garden of Eden, and in its Rose window the 'Law and the Prophets'. This 'mother cathedral' has the greatest treasury of stained glass of all churches in Britain.

Many cathedrals have magnificent Rose windows usually high at the west end of the building.

In Lincoln Cathedral's north transept there is a 'Dean's Eye' from 13th century glass, and look for 'The Sower' (1869) in 13th century form (see photos under 'Rose window').

Birmingham Anglican Cathedral has four great windows by Sir Edward Burne-Jones – inspired by medieval Christianity and art, these are masterpieces of stained glass.

St. Andrew Cathedral, Inverness, tracing its history back to St. Columba, has eight superb aisle windows by Hardman of Birmingham and also a richly coloured west window.

Similarly St. Mary's Glasgow has 12 windows at clerestory level, 10 in the nave and one in each transept, depicting lives of the apostles, made by Hardman of 1871-77 and with special use of 'white' in their designs.

Carlisle has its 14th century east window remarkably preserved despite all the destruction there.

Exeter's east window has glass from the 13th century that was re-set into the window in the 18th century, and by careful storage survived the Great Wars.

At Arundel RC Cathedral is a unique window of royal saints including Ethelbert, founder of Canterbury, and Edward the Confessor, King of England 1042-1066.

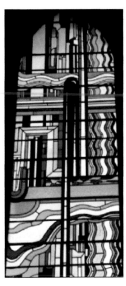

St. Mary's Episcopal Cathedral Edinburgh has a new magnificent window (right) that releases unusual features of light and colour into the building, designed by the sculptor, the late Sir Eduardo Paolozzi, who is also featured in the Dean Gallery of the National Galleries of Scotland.

At the west end of Lancaster RC Cathedral is this magnificent 'Te Deum' window from 1888, (below) made by Hardman of Birmingham, showing Christ seated in majesty in heaven and around Him, angels,

prophets and saints gather to sing His praise; that recalls the great hymn which begins with the words *'Te Deum laudamus'*, or *'We praise You, O God'*.

(St. Peter's was built between 1857 and 1859, originally as a new Catholic parish church for Lancaster. Catholics had been given freedom to build churches 30 years earlier in the Catholic Emancipation Act of 1829. In 1924

Pope Pius XI created the Diocese of Lancaster, and St. Peter's was chosen to be the cathedral church. In 2009 the cathedral celebrated its 150th anniversary).

Other notable examples of stained glass are at: Bath Abbey with a glorious east window, one of only a few not impeded by a reredos, and an 'Edgar' window for the Prince of Wessex, King of Mercia and first effective ruler of England from his coronation in 973 (the form of coronation still used today). Christ Church, Oxford with scenes from the life of Thomas Becket in its St. Lucy's Chapel; and one window in New College Oxford breaks all rules with a glorious nativity scene unlike any other, designed by Thomas Jervais in 1785 and painted by Sir Joshua Reynolds, with both appearing unrecognisable as shepherds. In Wells' north choir aisle there is a 1320 window of St. Michael fighting a dragon.

More modern examples are at:

Winchester: a 1914 window of Izaak Walton – author of 'The Compleat Angler', reading beside the River in a 'Study to be Quiet', and given by the fishermen of England; its west window was smashed by Roundheads in the Civil War: locals pieced it together but in a haphazard way so that it now appears to be modern abstract art.

St. Albans: a 1925 Sir Ninian Comper west window in 16th century style, to a considerable height;

Westminster Abbey: in its King Henry VII Chapel, a 1947 Battle of Britain window with figures of RAF aircrew and squadron badges designed and made by Hugh Easton;

Coventry: a 1962 major Baptistry window designed by John Piper and made by Patrick Reyntiens, one of a series in the cathedral;

Chichester: a 1978 window by French artist Marc Chagall, with dancing figures in animated gestures and with musical instruments, of Psalm 150 – "O praise God in his holiness".

The famous abbey at Buckfast also has this fine modern window made by the monks.

It is no exaggeration to say that 'stained glass' has undergone a revolution in the making and design, and with much damage during the Reformation and then the Civil War it is perhaps surprising that so much fine work remains.

Visitors to cathedrals should make a point of observing the stained glass windows that not only have a history but still do have stories to tell.

STALLS are special seats within the choir where clergy sat or stood during service. The stalls are often richly carved and fitted with misericords. It took a great carpenter, William Lyngewode, four years to carve the stalls at Winchester to create possibly the finest medieval carved stalls in Europe.

STATUES were numerous but mostly destroyed or defaced in medieval cathedrals and churches by puritans in the 17/18th centuries. However, there are many now in cathedrals mainly from commissions for special anniversaries or as memorials, both inside and outside the buildings. One of the most interesting (sometimes classified as a gargoyle) is that high on the exterior wall of Carlisle Cathedral of a laughing policeman, as a memorial. Others that have come to fame are:

John Hayward's *'Christ the Worker'* at Blackburn; Epstein's *'Michael the Archangel'* at Coventry; Eric Gill's *'The Blessed Trinity'* at Guildford; Sir Charles Wheeler's *'Madonna'* (dressed as a mill-girl) at Manchester;

Alan Durst's statuary (renewal) including the head of HM Queen Elizabeth, on the west front at Peterborough; and a *'St. Augustine'* in the door of the Rochester chapter house.

STEEPLE is a spire with bells in it, or a lofty structure especially a tower surmounted by a spire, rising above the roof of a church; see spire, steeple and tower.

STOUP is a container for holy water built into a wall, or free-standing near the west door on entry. Worshippers may dip their fingers into the holy water and bless themselves with the sign of the cross as a reminder of their baptism.

SURPLICE is the loose full-sleeved white-linen vestment descending to the knees or ankles, and worn over a cassock by clergy and by choristers at a service. See also robes and vestment.

TWENTY-THREE

TABLET: may be a small slab with inscription, perhaps known as a 'votive tablet', possibly as monument or memorial, but more normally recording an event or visit. At Derby for example, a fine commemorative tablet records the visit of HRH Prince Charles Edward Stuart, the 'Young Pretender', in December 1745 when his army had marched almost unhindered from Carlisle, camping around the town, before abandoning his march to London and return to Scotland where he was defeated at Culloden.

TAPESTRY is a thick, hand-woven textile fabric in which the design is formed by weft stitches (the transverse threads) across parts of warp. That at Coventry Cathedral is the most striking feature on entering the new cathedral; 72 feet high and designed by Graham Sutherland. Wherever you stand in the building, the eyes of Christ appear to be looking in your direction. Architect Basil Spence's original intention was to depict the Crucifixion but Provost Howard suggested that the subject be 'Christ in Majesty', and so this idea prevailed. Behind the high altar at Chichester is a brilliant modern tapestry by John Piper.

TESSELLATED PAVEMENT is unusual but mentioned here because the finest example is in the Roman Catholic

Westminster Cathedral in London. It is a floor covered with small blocks of mosaic consisting of marble and other material. See also mosaic for the Cosmati pavement in Westminster Abbey.

TOMB: as with Chantry, a gruesome topic for some, but a fascinating history for others as a burial place, usually for the high and mighty, but also for the humble and meek. A tomb can simply be a hole made in earth or rock to receive a dead human body, a grave, subterranean or other vault for the dead, or a sepulchral (funereal, gloomy or dismal) monument; thus a tombstone is a monumental stone placed over the grave, and that is what most people view in cathedrals. Some cathedrals have graves of past worshippers in the grounds of the building. In early times bodies were either buried in the ground or in stone coffins until a law was issued ensuring that all were buried in a woollen cloth. Modern day practice is that some cathedrals and churches, accept only cremated ashes for interment or for scattering in a reserved area of a memorial garden. It is the epitaph on the tomb or memorial that creates the main interest:

Canterbury with the Black Prince and St. Thomas Becket; Derby with Bess of Hardwick, founder of the Devonshire Family, and the tombstone (an 18th century medieval vault marker) of famous artist Joseph Wright; Durham with St. Bede and St. Cuthbert; Norwich with Nurse Cavell, a heroine from the First World War;

Peterborough with Catherine of Aragon (Henry VIIIs wife) and also Mary Queen of Scots (later re-interred in Westminster Abbey); Southwark with the first English poet,

John Gower; Winchester with Jane Austen, William Rufus and St. Swithun; Worcester with King John and Prince Henry; and York Minster with the tomb of Archbishop Grey, are just a few of so many notable tombs in cathedrals around Britain.

Westminster Abbey's Tomb of the Unknown Warrior (pictured here) is probably the best-known tomb – a poignant memorial to the soldiers who died in World War One.

On 11th November 1920, the unidentified body of a soldier was given a royal funeral and then buried in soil brought specially from the battlefields of France, beneath a marble stone quarried in Belgium. It is said that from time to time when the crowds have gone and the Abbey settles into quiet stillness, a ghostly soldier materialises alongside the tomb, and stands, head bowed, for a few minutes, before slowly dissolving into thin air.

In Chichester Cathedral rest the Earl and Countess of Arundel. Poet Philip Larkin, on seeing the effigies of the couple, side by side, was inspired to write 'An Arundel Tomb' with a final line: *"What will survive of us is love"*.

TOWER is a 'building of considerable elevation' or a tall, usually equilateral (especially square) or circular structure, often part of a church, and can house machinery, apparatus and operators (with the verb 'to tower'- to reach high above or over surroundings). See spire, steeple and tower.

Derby (left) has the third tallest tower after Canterbury and Liverpool.

In Exeter's north tower hangs the massive 'Peter Bell': the only bell in the tower, used as the clock bell, being struck on the outside by a hammer.

The south tower (below) houses the Cathedral's ring of 14 bells.

One can climb York Minster's 15th century tower with 275 steps, a test for the calf-muscles, for an impressive view across the city and Yorkshire, and one can gain also a bird's eye view of the minster.

Also very notable is the tower at Wells. (The original central tower was damaged by an earthquake in the 13th century and the rebuilding took 60 years but after only 20 years cracks appeared. In order to save the tower from collapse the master mason, William Joy, built the 'scissors arches' that are still an important and attractive part of the design, and the hidden buttresses in the upper parts. Some 700 years later those measures have preserved the tower).

Blackburn Cathedral has an unusual lantern from its tower known locally as 'the lighthouse' especially when illuminated, but possibly the most famous now is the lantern tower of the Liverpool RC Cathedral with crowning pinnacles over 52 feet high with diagonal struts to strengthen them against the wind.

TRACERY in Gothic architecture is the slender moulded stone bar intersecting to form patterns at the top of a window, used much in the 13th to 16th centuries, and as flowering tracery assumed as 'grid-iron' pattern, mainly because it framed the popular pictures in stained glass windows of saints.

Carlisle's east window contains one of the best examples of decorated tracery, and in addition the delicate carved capitals in the quire depict the seasons.

TRANSEPT: in any cruciform (cross-shaped) cathedral, the transept is the transverse arm north and south of the crossing that usually houses memorials, and chapels, and often now special displays. Canterbury, Lincoln, Salisbury and Worcester have an additional pair of eastern transepts, named double transepts. In the south transept of Winchester Cathedral is the grave of Izaac Walton, of '*Compleat Angler*' fame; in the north aisle the grave of Jane Austen, and many other treasures. Dominating the north transept of St. Paul's, London is the famous painting '*The Light of the World*' by William Holman Hunt, and in the south transept monuments of explorer Sir Robert Scott, naval hero Admiral Nelson leaning on an anchor, and landscape artist JMW Turner. At Portsmouth the transepts retain some Norman features, such as lancet windows and arched recesses, with the later northern transept containing the slightly later cusped windows and arch. This is all that remains of the medieval church, but enough survives to indicate it was a church of the finest quality.

The unusual positioning of the organ in Worcester's south transept.

TREASURY is the room(s) that displays the historic silver of chalice, patens and plates, vestments and other treasures. Chichester, Derby, Norwich and St. Paul's London have outstanding treasures. At Durham the Treasury is beneath the Library, displaying many artefacts that have played a part in its long history, including the priceless relics associated with St. Cuthbert.

A medieval painted angel in the Treasury at Norwich.

In the treasury at York is a unique and ancient, elephant tusk drinking horn with cats and unicorns, given by a Viking, Ulf.

Whilst individual cathedrals have fine treasures, it is worth visiting the British Library, located between King's Cross and Euston Stations in London, to view a number of great treasures gathered together on display, that include:

The Lindisfarne Gospel of 698-720 by artist Monk Eadfrith, Bishop of Lindisfarne, dedicated to God and St. Cuthbert.

Other sacred Illuminated Texts of Islam, Judaism, Daoism of Japan, and from India.

A Bestiary from Salisbury of 1230; the *De Lisle Psalter* of London 1310; *the St. Omer Psalter* of Norfolk 1330.

The Sherborne Missal of 1400 made for the Benedictine Abbey of Sherborne, Dorset, that is vast in volume and weighs over three stone. Beautifully illustrated, it includes a Calendar of Feast Days, of which the most important are coloured in red (and in blue) leading to the phrase 'red letter days' marking important events such as Christ's birth. This missal contains also all the music needed for any Mass that the priest would chant or sing.

TREFOIL means a 'three-leaved object', either a carved ornament or a panel or an opening in tracery.

TRIFORIUM is the internal wall above the arcade and below the clerestory in a cathedral, often known as 'the blind storey' as a contrast to the 'clerestory' because this is pierced with windows, whereas the triforium is the dark or blind space over the aisle. As a galleried arcade it looks like a 'blind-storey' – a row of window frames without window openings.

TRIPTYCH: a carving or picture on three panels with sides able to fold over to the centre, especially used as an altar piece.

This glorious triptych is in the Lancaster RC Cathedral, acting as a reredos. Designed by Sir Giles Gilbert Scott, whose many significant works include the Liverpool Anglican Cathedral and the Albert Memorial in London, it was placed above the altar in 1909, removed in the 1970s and restored to its position in 1995.

The Westminster RC Cathedral houses a magnificent 'Chapel of the Apostle to the Gentiles', with an apse of Turkish marble and an altar of white marble similar to that used in the Parthenon in Athens where St. Paul preached, along with the gilt-bronze triptych of St. Paul. (See photo under apse). Carlisle has a 16th century Flemish triptych as an altarpiece in its St. Wilfred's Chapel.

TYMPANUM (plural, tympana) is the semi-circular or triangular decorative wall surface over an entrance bounded by a lintel and arch, that often contains sculptures or other ornaments. In Greek and Christian architecture it usually contained religious scenes. (Bands of moulding surrounding the tympanum are referred to as the archivolt.)

At Southwell Minster only the tympanum in the north transept remains from when the Normans began rebuilding the Saxon church in 1108, completing the nave in 1150.

A crowning glory of Worcester Cathedral is a heraldic eagle that forms part of the richly carved and decorated tympanum, designed by one Thomas White in 1722.

In Edinburgh there is record of a modest parish church by the year 854, subsequently re-consecrated and named in honour of the patron saint of the town, St. Giles in France, probably due to the ancient ties between Scotland and France. According to legend, Giles was accidentally wounded by a huntsman in pursuit of a hind and, after his death in the early 8th century, there were dedicated to him hospitals and safe houses for cripples, beggars and lepers throughout England and Scotland. St. Giles is usually depicted protecting a hind from an arrow, which had pierced his own body, a fine relief which rests in the tympanum over the west (main) doors of St. Giles' Cathedral in Edinburgh.

TWENTY-FOUR

UNDERCROFT is a crypt without windows, but both crypt and undercroft are used to describe rooms below ground as at York Minster and St. Paul's London.

VAULT or vaulting, is the arched roof, continuous arch or a series of arches whose joints radiate from a central point or line. The ribbed vault in Durham Cathedral (left) was completed as early as 1133. It was the first in Europe, and its slightly pointed arches perhaps look forward to Gothic style.

At Exeter (below) the view of the nave and quire vaulting from the west end is unforgettable – the longest continuous piece of medieval vaulting in the world described as 'an avenue of palms'.

The cathedral advises visitors to view the vault on a bright day and with a good pair of binoculars!

The Thistle chapel in St. Giles' Cathedral in Edinburgh is a must-see: Gothic style with fan-vaulted ceiling, carvings and heraldic details and, of course, the famous John Knox was minister here in 1560, and Parliament has also met here: history indeed.

At Arundel RC Cathedral there is an outstanding nave and a sanctuary with high vaulting, typical of the French gothic era. At Bath Abbey the fan vaulting over the nave is a Victorian copy of the original Tudor design. Bath's Heritage Vault is splendid, housing an engaging story and display of its heritage, and illustrating many of the decorative stone features of the abbey.

A vault can also be an arched cellar or subterranean chamber as place of storage, or for internment by burial beneath a church.

VESTMENT is an interesting word linked with vest – to furnish a person with authority, powers, or property; or a waistcoat. It is an official garment for clergy and choristers worn during divine service, and especially the chasuble – the long sleeveless vestment worn by a priest and minister during Mass or Eucharist. (Enter the term 'chasuble' into the web and over one million entries appear, not only in description but in sales of such garments.)

VESTRY is a room within or attached to a church which is used to store vestments or other items used in worship, and usually of a sufficient size to allow those using vestments to change into them, and thus in England and elsewhere often used for meetings dealing with the administration of the local parish.

In Welsh chapels it is often the location of a tea served to the congregation, particularly family members after a funeral, when the congregation returns to the chapel after the burial or cremation.

In some parts of the Anglican Communion, the term 'vestry' continues to be used for a body of lay members elected by the congregation or parish to run the secular business of the parish. The vestry may have additional functions, including selection of the vicar or rector of the church, who is usually an ex-officio member of the vestry and may chair its meetings. The leading lay members of the vestry are generally the wardens, perhaps vicar's warden and people's warden.

TWENTY-FIVE

WEST FRONT is the stonework housing the main entrance to the cathedral, although nowadays another entrance may be used by visitors for convenience (and for collection of entrance fee and donation).

The west front is important also for its elaborate carvings on the door often alongside the grandeur of the building, as at Wells. Begun in 1215, and when completed displaying the largest collection of figurative statues in the western world, the west front at Wells depicted the history as told in the Bible, and was painted with brilliant strong colours. Now it is just bare stone but still glorious. (See also facade.)

The west front of Peterborough Cathedral

Other major west fronts are at Bath, Bury St. Edmunds, Canterbury, Exeter, Hereford, Inverness, Lincoln, London St. Paul's, Peterborough, Rochester, Salisbury, York, and the more modern at Coventry.

That at Llandaff is from 1220 and one of the most outstanding medieval works of *art* in Wales.

POSTSCRIPT

Engaging in a tour of all cathedrals in Britain, and some on the continent, really does open one's eyes, ears and mind. Cathedrals are not unique in that there are many in Britain and abroad, but each cathedral has at least one feature unique to that building. Learning more of unusual features in a cathedral, abbey, minster or church also opens one's eyes and mind to some of these features seen in other remarkable buildings, such as historic houses, even in older theatres and cinemas, and in cities or towns where one may live or visit, such as in Edinburgh with its notable buildings and with many examples of arches, columns and domes, to name just a few. I have always believed it is important to look up in a city or town and view the unusual. We tend not to do so, being afraid perhaps that we might trip, or of what we might step into, inadvertently, on the pavement.

It is quite remarkable what one misses on a building by not looking up – some of the best features are usually at the top.

Similarly, at a cathedral, look around and up, and on entering after reflection, look up and then ahead before moving around. 'Up' is usually rewarding especially when there is a carved ceiling (perhaps like the upturned hull of a boat reaching heavenwards), except in a few cathedrals such as the Roman Catholic Cathedral at Westminster London or the St. Mary's Episcopal Cathedral in Edinburgh where the ceilings are rather dark and cold. Then, look ahead and view the rich colour before even commencing the tour around. The solidity and decoration of stonework and the richness of colour, natural and created, are crucial and exciting, sometimes overwhelming.

Light has always been a token of splendour, before artificial light became important. If light is seen as a spiritual aspect or splendour then we may see it is a sign of heavenly grace. It is certainly crucial. Too much stained glass leads to too little light; a blend of stained and natural glass and the patterns of light create vitality and warmth to enrich the interior. Let the light shine: reflect, appreciate and enjoy... and perhaps wonder as one of the curious.

A choir entering the quire provides colour to a ceremonial activity and, dare I say it, warmth to the liturgy. In a similar way the organ producing music in a cathedral, even in practice, creates life in the building.

The best cathedral choirs heard on tour?

Without doubt, the Choir of Westminster Roman Catholic Cathedral; with all of the Anglican cathedrals being very special on the day of hearing. All the cathedral choirs are absolutely superb. The most enjoyable Evensong was at Chichester where the style and blend of ministers, choir and organ in the music and speech was very, very pleasing. Second, possibly, was at St. David's Cathedral in Wales, a glorious setting on St. David's Day with fine music and outstanding sermon by the bishop.

To hear a choir of over 300 at a Festival Evensong at Ely Cathedral was unique. Bath Abbey, Ripon and Salisbury Cathedral Girls' Choirs produced delightful performances in special services, and mention must be made of all the choirs at Llandaff Cathedral, Cardiff. Living in Edinburgh I have the privilege of listening regularly to the choir at St. Mary's Episcopal Cathedral that maintains a very high standard.

It is unfair really to select a 'favourite' as one can easily hear a choir on an 'off-day' especially when one remembers the exacting and large amount of music that a cathedral choir performs week in and week out, and the exacting standard to which the clergy, director of music and organist aspire.

All the cathedral visits created a wonderful experience.

A visit to each cathedral, abbey and minster highlights the tremendous and challenging cost of maintenance, repair and restoration without even taking into account the cost of the services and administration. Each church seems to have an appeal for funds, often of a staggering amount to the average visitor. It was worrying to read during this period of threats to the upkeep of such buildings by cutbacks in government support of the buildings. No one would expect government to support financially the worship and administration, but it is surely an important and essential part of government activity to support heritage of a precious nature, and not by relying solely on sources such as the Lottery.

News in July 2010 (Daily Telegraph 18.7.2010) that the Wolfson Foundation was giving a lead to all concerned with a grant of £500,000 for repairs to fabric of cathedrals (to help fill the gap left by withdrawal of government English Heritage funding) is welcome but it does not overcome the problem. It was reported that "an alarming number of cathedrals are crumbling, with masonry falling from the walls, roofs leaking and pillars being held together with duct tape".

A fascinating report is that of the Archbishops' Council Cathedral and Church Buildings Division, titled "Cathedrals Fabric Commission for England Annual review 2009". This gives an overview of grants made and for the breadth of purposes used in cathedrals (see Further Reading). A brief account of history shows us the relevance and importance of such buildings to the heritage and life of the nations, and it is to be hoped that governments in all countries of Britain will take a more tangible and supportive role in ensuring that these famous, historic and valuable assets are assisted more constructively and generously.

Some people will dispute that argument especially quoting the disagreements within the different denominations. It is a complicated history, and even more so about churches outside of the British Isles. However, any disagreements should not override the prime fact that cathedrals and other churches are and will be historic, and a significant feature of the country's heritage. They deserve adequate protection.

We must remember that individuals are free to worship in their church of choosing, and not to believe or worship if they choose not to do so. Even though there are still healthy differences of opinion in the several churches there is also much sharing of belief, customs and practice, knowledge and opinion. More learning is challenging but worthwhile, for there is so much history within cathedrals and abbeys. There are several fine books (and websites) on cathedrals and other churches, especially of an architectural nature, but those given below are of general interest to the general reader.

Thank you for reading and I hope the content will have stimulated you to visit, enjoy and to learn more, and perhaps support the fine, outstanding cathedrals, abbeys, minsters, chapels and churches in our heritage.

FURTHER READING

A Little Book of:
Gargoyles. 1998.ISBN 1 85410 561 2
Misericords. 1998. ISBN 1 85410 562 0
Stained Glass. 1998. ISBN 1 85410 564 7
The Green Man. 1998. ISBN 185410 563 9
All by Mike Harding and published by Aurum Press Ltd,
25 Bedford Avenue, London WC1B 3AT.
Guided by a Stonemason. Thomas Maude 1997. IB Tauris
Publishers. ISBN 1 86064 039 7
Cathedral Architecture: the Pitkin Guide. Pitkin
Publishing.
2001. reprinted. ISBN 978 1 84165 076 0.
Cathedral Architecture. Pitkin Pictorials. 1973.
ISBN 85372 083 5 (out of print but worth acquiring).
Stained Glass: the Pitkin Guide. Pitkin Publishing. 2001.
reprinted.
The Green Man: the Pitkin Guide. Pitkin Publishing.
2001.
reprinted. ISBN 978 1 84165 045 6
Scottish Cathedrals. Richard Fawcett. Historic Scotland.
1997. ISBN 0 7134 8188 9
Cathedrals of England, Scotland and Wales.
Paul Johnson. 1990. Weiden and Nicholson.
ISBN 0 297 83013 9

Cathedrals & Abbeys of England. Stephen Platten. 2005.
Jarrold Publishing. ISBN 0 7117 1003 1
Abbeys & Monasteries. Derry Brabbs. Weidenfeld &
Nicholson. 1999. ISBN 0 297 824 953
*The Book of Books: The radical impact of the King James
Bible 1611-2011*. Melvyn Bragg. Hodder & Straughton.
2011. ISBN 978 1 4447055157

*Cathedrals Fabric Commission for England Annual
Review 2009* (covering all Anglican Cathedrals in England).
Archbishops' Council Cathedral and Church Buildings
Division. Janet Gough, Secretary, Church House, Great Smith
Street, London SW1P 3AZ. (Tel: 020 7898 1866). Available on
website: www.cofe.anglican.org/about/Cathandchurchbuild
email: webmaster@c-of-e.org.uk

Other Reading of interest:

God's Big Instruction Book. Julie Mabey. Oneworld
Publications, Oxford. ISBN 1-85168-170-1
John Betjeman: On Churches. Jonathan Glancey.
Methuen. 2007. ISBN. 13: 978 0 413 77651 8

Each cathedral has a guide book, some published by
the cathedral, most by Pitkin Publishing or Jarrold
Publishing.

There are several books on each cathedral but one in
particular is an excellent read describing the trials and
tribulations, and success:

The Building of Liverpool Cathedral. Peter Kennerley. Carnegie Publishing 1991. ISBN 0-948789-72-7

Each main denomination with cathedrals has its own website but to learn more of the history of the several churches with cathedrals, from an independent review, see the Wikipedia website under the following titles: Church of England; Church in Wales;
Church of Ireland; Scottish Episcopal Church; Church of Scotland;
Catholic Church; Roman Catholicism in Ireland;
Roman Catholic Churches in Northern Ireland.

Other interesting websites:

Cathedrals (Pilgrims Association)
www.cathedralsplus.org.uk

Cathedral Architecture:
www.library.thinkquest.org/10098/cathedrals.
www.karenswhimsy.com
www.wordiq.com
en.wikipedia.org/wiki/Architecture_of_cathedrals_and_ great churches (also: type in the name of the cathedral plus 'architecture' e.g: Canterbury Cathedral architecture)

Cathedral Buildings: en.wikipedia.org/wiki/Cathedral
Cathedral Communications Ltd:
www.buldingconservation.com

British Institute of Organ Studies:
www.duresme.org.uk/bios (& for links to other Organ sites)

Incorporated Association of Organists:
www.iao.org.uk

Bells and bell-ringing:
en.wikipedia.org/wiki/Campanology

Central Council of Church Bell-ringers:
www.cccbr.org.uk

UK Cathedral Music Links:
www.cathedralmusiclinks.org.uk (an excellent site)

Choirs: en.wikipedia.org/wiki/Choir
www.churchmusic.org.uk

History of choristers: www.ofchoristers.net

Vestments: www.kencollins.com
& en.wikipedia.org/wiki/Vestment

$\mathcal{APPENDIX} \mathcal{A}$

(Details are subject to change; always check the website
for updates. Correct at June 2011)

ANGLICAN CATHEDRALS in ENGLAND
(Church of England)

Birmingham
(St. Philip) Colmore Rowe, Birmingham.
B3 2QB. 0121 2621840.
email: enquiries@birminghamcathedral.
com
web: www.birminghamcathedral.com

Blackburn
(St. Mary the Virgin) Cathedral Close,
Blackburn.
BB1 5AA. 01254 503090.
email: dean@blackburncathedral.co.uk
web: www.blackburncathedral.com

Bradford
(St. Peter) 1 Stott Hill, Bradford.
BD1 4EH.
01274 777720.
email: info@bradfordcathedral.org
web: www.bradfordcathedral.co.uk

Bristol
(Holy and Undivided Trinity)
College Green, Bristol.
B51 5TJ.
0117 9264879.
email: reception@bristol-cathedral.co.uk
web: www.bristol-cathedral.co.uk

Bury St. Edmunds -
St. Edmundsbury-
(St. James).
Abbey House, Angel Hill,
Bury St. Edmunds. IP33 1LS.
01284 748720.
email: cathedral@stedscathedral.co.uk
web: www.stedscathedral.co.uk

Canterbury	(Church of Christ) 11 The Precincts, Canterbury. CT1 2EH. 01227 762862. email: enquiries@canterbury-cathedral.org web: www.canterbury-cathedral.org
Carlisle	(Holy and Undivided Trinity) 7 The Abbey, Carlisle, Cumbria. CA3 8TZ. 01228 548151. email:office@carlislecathedral.org.uk web: www.carlislecathedral.org.uk
Chelmsford	(St. Mary, St. Peter and St. Cedd) New Street, Chelmsford. CM1 1TY 01245 294489. email: office@chelmsfordcathedral.org.uk web: www.chelmsfordcathedral.org.uk
Chester	(Christ and the Blessed Virgin Mary) 12 Abbey Square, Chester. CH1 2HU. 01244 324756. email: office@chestercathedral.com web: www.chestercathedral.com
Chichester	(Holy Trinity) The Royal Chantry, Cathedral Cloisters, Chichester. PO19 1PX. 01243 782595. email: enquiry@chichestercathedral.org.uk web: chichestercathedral.org.uk
Coventry	(St.Michael's) 1 Hill Top, Coventry. CV1 5AB. 024 76521200. email: (direct from web) web: www.coventrycathedral.org.uk
Derby	(Collegiate Church of All Saints'). 18-19 Iron Gate, Derby. DE1 3GP. 01332 341201. email: office@derbycathedral.org web: www.derbycathedral.org
Durham	(Christ, the Blessed Mary the Virgin and St. Cuthbert) The Chapter Office, The College, Durham. DH1 3EH. 0191 3864266. email: enquiries@durhamcathedral.co.uk web: www.durhamcathedral.co.uk
Ely	(Holy and Undivided Trinity). The College. Ely. CB7 4DL. 01353 667735. email: receptionist@cathedral.ely.anglican.org web: www.elycathedral.org

Exeter	(St.Peter). 1 The Cloisters. Exeter EX1 1HS. 01392 255573. email: reception@exeter-cathedral.org.uk web: exeter-cathedral.org.uk
Gloucester	(St. Peter and the Undivided Trinity). 12 The College Green, Gloucester. GL1 2LX. 0145 2528095. email: (direct from web). web: www.gloucestercathedral.org.uk
Guildford	(The Holy Spirit). Stag Hill, Guildford. GU2 7UP. 01483 547860. email: reception@guildford-cathedral.org web: www.guildford-cathedral.org
Hereford	(St. Mary the Virgin & St. Ethelbert the King). 5 College Cloisters, Hereford. HR1 2NG. 01432 374202. email: office@herefordcathedral.org web: www.herefordcathedral.org
Leicester	(St. Martin). 21 St. Martin's, Leicester. LE1 5DE. 0116 2487400. email: leicestercathedral@leccofe.org web: www.cathedral.leicester.anglican.org
Lichfield	(The Blessed Virgin Mary and St. Chad). 19a The Close, Lichfield. WS13 7LD. 01543 306100. email: (direct from web). web: www.lichfield-cathedral.org
Lincoln	(the Blessed Virgin Mary). 4 Priorygate Lincoln LN2 1PL. 01522 561600. email: visitors@lincolncathedral.com web: www.lincolncathedral.com
Liverpool	(Cathedral Church of Christ) St. James's Mount, Liverpool Merseyside. L1 7AZ. 0151 7096271. email: info@liverpoolcathedral.org.uk web: www.liverpoolcathedral.org.uk

London	(St. Paul) St.Paul's Churchyard, London EC4M 8AD. 020 72468537 email: chapter@stpaulscathedral.org.uk web: www.stpauls.co.uk
London	(Southwark Collegiate Church of St. Saviour and St. Mary Overie). London Bridge, Southwark. London SE1 9DA. 020 73676700. email: cathedral@southwark.anglican.org web: www.cathedralsouthwark.anglican.org
Manchester	(St. Mary, St. Denys & St. George). Victoria Street, Manchester. M3 1SX. 0161 833 2220. email: (direct from Web). web: www.manchestercathedral.org
Newcastle	(St. Nicholas). St. Nicholas Churchyard. Newcastle-upon-Tyne, Tyne & Wear. NE1 1PF. 0191 232 1939. email: office@stnicnewcastle.co.uk web: www.stnicholascathedral.co.uk
Norwich	(Holy and Undivided Trinity). 12 The Close, Norwich, NR1 4DH. 01603 218300. email:reception@cathedral.org.uk web: www.cathedral.org.uk
Oxford	(Church of Christ). Christ Church, Oxford. OX1 1DP. 01865 27616. email: cathedral@chch.ox.ac.uk web: www.chch.ox.ac.uk
Peterborough	(St. Peter, St. Paul and St. Andrew). Minster Precincts, Peterborough. PE1 1XS. 01733 355300. email: info@peterboroughcathedral.org.uk web: www.peterborough-cathedral.org.uk
Portsmouth	(St. Thomas). St. Thomas's Street, Old Portsmouth. PO1 2HA. 0239 2823300. email: enquiries@portsmouthcathedral.org.uk web: www.portsmouthcathedral.org.uk

Ripon	(St. Peter and St. Wilfred). Liberty Court House, Minster Road, Ripon. HG4 1QS. 01765 603462 email: postmaster@riponcathedral.org.uk web: www.riponcathedral.org.uk
Rochester	(Christ and the Blessed Virgin Mary). Garth House, The Precinct, Rochester. ME1 1SX. 01634 843366 email: (direct from web). web: www.rochestercathedral.org
St. Albans	(St. Alban). Sumpter Yard, St. Albans. AL1 1BY. 01727 860780. email: mail@stalbanscathedral.org.uk web: www.stalbanscathedral.org
St. Edmundsbury	(see Bury St. Edmunds)
Salisbury	(St. Mary). 6 The Close, Salisbury. SP1 2EF. 01722 555 113 or 120. email: (direct from Web). web: www.salisburycathedral.org.uk
Sheffield	(St.Peter and St.Paul). Church Street, Sheffield, South Yorkshire. S1 1HA. 0114 2753434. email: enquiries@sheffield-cathedral.org.uk web: www.sheffield-cathedral.org.uk
Southwell	(The Blessed Virgin Mary). Southwell Minster, Church Street, Southwell. NG25 0HD. 01636 812649 email: office@southwellminster.org.uk web: www.southwellminster.org
Truro	(The Blessed Virgin Mary). 14 St. Mary's Street, Truro. TR1 2AF. 01872 276782. email: (direct from web). web: www.trurocathedral.org.uk
Wakefield	(All Saints). 8-10 Westmorland Street, Wakefield, WF1 1PJ. email: admin@wakefield-cathedral.org.uk web: www.wakefieldcathedral.org.uk
Wells	(St. Andrew). Cathedral Green, Wells. BA5 2UE. 01749 674483. email: (direct from Web) web: www.wellscathedral.org.uk

Winchester	(Holy Trinity, St. Peter, St. Paul and St. Swithun). 9 The Close, Winchester, SO23 9LS. 01962 857200. email: (direct from web) web: www.winchester-cathedral.org.uk
Worcester	(Christ and the Blessed Virgin the Mary of Worcester). 8 College Yard, Worcester. WR1 2LA. 01905 732900. email: info@worcestercathedral.org.uk web: www.worcestercathedral.co.uk
York Minster	(St.Peter). Church House, Ogleforth, York. YO1 7JN. 0844 9390011. email: info@yorkminster.org web: www.yorkminster.org
London Westminster Abbey	Although not a cathedral it is included here in view of its special history and attraction: (Collegiate Church of St.Peter). 20 Dean's Yard, London SW1P 3PA. 020 72225152 email: (direct from web) web: www.Westminster-abbey.org
Isle of Man	(St. German). Peel. Isle of Man. IM5 1HH. (Province of York). 01624 842608. email: subdean.sodor@gmail.com web: www.cofe.anglican.org
Gibraltar	(Holy Trinity). Cathedral Square, Gibraltar. (Province of Canterbury). 00350 20075745. email: anglicangib@gibtelecom.net web: www.gibconnect.com

ANGLICAN CATHEDRALS in NORTHERN IRELAND
(Church of Ireland)

Armagh

(St. Patrick). 43 Abbey Street, Armagh. 028375 23142
email: admin@armaghpubliclibrary.co.uk
web: www.stpatricks-cathedral.org

Belfast

(St. Anne). Donegall Street, Belfast. Co. Antrim. BT1 2HB. 028 90328332.
email: admin@belfastcathedral.org
web: www.belfastcathedral.org

Derry

(St. Columb). London Street, Londonderry. BT48 6RQ. 028 71267313.
email: st.columbs@ic24.net
web: www.stcolumbscathedral.org

Down

(St.Patrick) English Street, Downpatrick BT30 6AB. 028 44614922
email:info@downcathedral.org
web: www.downcathedral.org

ANGLICAN CATHEDRALS in SCOTLAND
(Scottish Episcopal Church)

Aberdeen

(St. Andrew). 28 King Street, Aberdeen. AB24 5AX. 01224 640119.
email:cathedral@aberdeen.anglican.org
web:
www.cathedral@aberdeen.anglican.org

Cathedral of the Isles:(Collegiate Church of the Holy Spirit).
The College, Millport, Isle of Cumbrae. KA28 0HE. 01475 530353.
email: cathedral_cumbrae@btconnect.com
web: www.island-retreats.org

Dundee

(St. Paul).1 High Street, Dundee. DD1 1TD. 01382 224486
email: info@dundeecathedral.org.uk
Web: www.stpaulscathedraldundee.org

Edinburgh	(St. Mary). Palmerston Place, Edinburgh. EH12 5AW. 0131 2256293. email:office@cathedral.net web: www.cathedral.net
Glasgow	(St. Mary the Virgin). 300 Great Western Road, Glasgow. G4 9JB. 0141 3396691 email: (direct from web). web: www.thecathedral.org.uk
Inverness	(St. Andrew). 15 Ardross Street, Inverness. IV3 5NS. 01463 233535. email: canonalexgordon@btconnect.com web: www.invernesscathedral.co.uk
Oban	(St. John the Divine). George Street, Oban. PA34 5DJ. 01631 56232. email:provostoban@argyll.anglican.org web: www.st-johns-cathedral-oban-org.uk
Perth	(St. Ninian). North Methven Street, Perth, Perthshire. PH1 5PP. 01738 632053. email: office@perthcathedral.co.uk web: www.perthcathedral.co.uk

CATHEDRALS of the CHURCH of SCOTLAND

(not technically cathedrals now but historic churches, in this Presbyterian Church that does not have bishops)

Aberdeen	(St. Machar). The Chanonry, Old Aberdeen, Aberdeen. AB24 1RQ. 01224 485988. email: office@stmachar.com web: www.stmachar.com
Brechin	(Holy Trinity). Church Street, Brechin, Angus. DD9 6EU. 01356 629360. email: office@brechincathedral.org web: www.brechincathedral.org

Dornoch	(St. Mary). Cathedral Square. Dornach. IV25 3SJ. web: www.dornoch-cathedral.com
Dunblane	(St. Blane). The Cross, Dunblane. FK15 0AQ. 01786 825388. email: none web: www.dunblanecathedral.org.uk
Dunkeld	(St. Columba). Cathedral Street. Dunkeld. Perthshire. PH8 0AN. 01350 727614. email: minister@dunkeldcathedral.org.uk web: www.dunkeldcathedral.org.uk
Edinburgh	(St. Giles). St.Giles' Cathedral, Edinburgh EH1 1RE. 0131 2254363 email: info@stgilescathedral.org.uk web: www.stgilescathedral.org.uk
Glasgow	(St. Mungo). Castle Street, Glasgow. |G4. 0141 5528198. email: info@glasgowcathedral.org.uk web: www.glasgow-cathedral.com & www.GlasgowCathedral.org.uk
Lismore	(St. Moluag). Isle of Lismore, near Oban. (Known as Lismore Parish Church). Lismore PA34 5UL.
Kirkwall	(St. Magnus). St.Magnus Cathedral, Kirkwall, Isle of Orkney. 0560 1963372 email: cathedral@orkney.gov.uk web: www.stmagnus.org

ANGLICAN CATHEDRALS in WALES

| Bangor | (St. Deiniol). Gwynedd. North Wales. LL57 1LH. 01248 353983. email: martinbrown@churchinwales.org. uk web: esgobaeth.bangordiocese.org/cathedral or www.churchinwales.org.uk) |

Brecon	(formerly Brecon Priory: St. John the Evangelist) The Cathedral Close, Brecon, Powys. LD3 9DP. 01874 623857. email: admin@breconcathedral.org.uk web: www.breconcathedral.org.uk
Llandaff, Cardiff	(SS. Peter and Paul, Dyfrig, Teilo and Euddogwy). Llandaff, Cardiff CF5 2LA. 029 2056 4554 email: office@llandaffcathedral.org.uk web: www.llandaffcathedral.org.uk
Newport (Monmouth)	(St.Woolos). Stow Hill, Newport, NP20 4EA. 01633 212077. email: stwooloscathedral@btinternet.com web: www.churchinwales.org.uk
St. Asaph Cathedral	High Street, St. Asaph. Denbighshire. North Wales. LL17 0RD. 01745 582245. email: (direct from web). web: churchinwales.org.uk/asaph/cathedral
St. David's Cathedral	The Close, St. David's, Pembrokeshire, SA62 6RH. 01437 720202 email: info@stdavidscathedral.org.uk web: www.stdavidscathedral.org.uk

ROMAN CATHOLIC CATHEDRALS in England:

London Westminster	(The Most Precious Blood of our Lord Jesus Christ) 42 Francis Street, London SW1P 1QW. 020 77989055. email: chreception@redow.org.uk web: www.westminstercathedral.org.uk
London Southwark	(St. George). Cathedral House, Westminster Bridge Road, London SE1 7HY. 020 79285256. email: info@southwark-rc-cathedral.org.uk web: southwark-rc-cathedral-org.uk

London	(Ukranian Cathedral of the Holy Family in Exile). 21 Binney Street, off Duke Street, Mayfair, London 020 76291534. (temporarily closed). See various entries under title on websites.
Aldershot	(St. Michael and St. George) (Bishopric of the British Armed Forces). Queens Avenue, Aldershot. GU11 2BY. 01252 347464. website www.gcatholic.com
Arundel	(Our Lady and St. Philip Howard). Parsons Hill, Arundel. BN18 9AY. 01903 882297. email: aruncath1@aol.com web: www.arundelcathedral.org
Birmingham	(Basilica of St. Chad). Queensway, Birmingham. B4 6EU. 0121 236 2251. email: reception@rc-birmingham.org web: www.stchadscathedral.org.uk
Brentwood	(St.Mary and St.Helen). Ingrave Road, Brentwood, Essex. CM15 8AT. 01277 265235. email: (not given). web: www.cathedral-brentwood.org
Bristol	(St. Peter and St.Paul). Clifton Park, Bristol, BS8 3BX. 0117 9738411. email: (see web) web: www.cliftoncathedral.org.uk
Lancaster	(St. Peter). Balmoral Road, Lancaster. LA1 3BT. 01524 384820. email: clergy@lancastercathedral.org.uk web: www.lancastercathedral.org.uk
Leeds	(St. Anne). Great George Street, Leeds LS2 8BE. 0113 2454545 email: cathedral@dioceseofleeds.org.uk web: www.leedscathedral.org.uk
Liverpool	(Christ the King). Mount Pleasant, Liverpool. L3 5TQ. 0151 7099222. email:enquiries@metcathedral.org.uk web: www.liverpoolmetrocathedral.org.uk

Middlesbrough	(St. Mary). Dalby Way, Coulby Newham, Middlesbrough. TS8 0TW. 01642 597750. email: Parish@middlesbroughrccathedral.org web: middlesbroughrccathedral.org
Newcastle	(St. Mary). Clayton Street West, Newcastle upon Tyne NE1 5HH. 0191 2326953. email: office@stmaryscathedral.org.uk web: www.stmaryscathedral.org.uk
Northampton	(Our Lady and St. Thomas). Kingsthorpe Road, Northampton. NN2 6AG. 01604 714556. email: office@northamptoncathedral.org web: www.northamptoncathedral.org
Norwich	(St. John the Baptist). Unthank Road, Norwich, Norfolk. NR2 2PA. 01603 624615. email: enq@sjbcathedral.org.uk web: www.sjbcathedral.org.uk
Nottingham	(St. Barnabas). Derby Road, Nottingham. 0115 9539839. email: generalenquiries@ stbarnabascathedral.org.uk web: www.stbarnabascathedral.org.uk
Plymouth	(St. Mary and St. Boniface). 45 Cecil Street, Plymouth, Devon. PL1 5HW. 01752 662537. email: parish@plymouthcathedral.co.uk web: www.plymouthcathedral.co.uk
Portsmouth	(St. John the Evangelist). Edinburgh Road, Portsmouth. PO1 3HG. 023 92826170 email: info@ portsmouthcatholiccathedral.org.uk web: portsmouthcatholiccathedral.com

Salford	(St. John the Evangelist). 250 Chapel Street, Salford. M3 5LL. 0161 8340333. email: cathedral@salforddiocese.org web: www.dioceseofsalford.org.uk/cathedral
Sheffield	(St. Marie). Norfolk Street, Sheffield. S1 2JB. 0114 2722522. email: office@stmariecathedral.org web: stmariecathedral.org/drupal
Shrewsbury	(Our Lady Help of Christians and St. Peter of Alcantara). 11 Belmont Street, Shrewsbury. SY1 1TE. 0174 3362366. email: admin@shrewsburycathedral.co.uk web: www.shrewsbury cathedral.org

Northern Ireland:

Armagh	(St. Patrick). Cathedral Road, Armagh. BT61 7QY. 028 37522045. email: admin@aracoeli.com web: www.armagharchdiocese.org/ stpatrickscathedral
Belfast	(St. Peter). St. Peter's Square South, Belfast. BT12 4BU. 028 90327573. email: stpetersbelfast@hotmail.co.uk web: www.stpeterscathedralbelfast.com
Newry	(St.Patrick and St. Colman). Newry. Co Down. BT35 6PN web: www.dromorediocese.org

Scotland:

Aberdeen	(St. Mary). Huntley Street, Aberdeen. 01224 640280. email: abdn1.cathedral@btconnect.com web: ww.stmaryscathedralaberdeen.org
Ayr	(St. Margaret). 27 John Street, Ayr. KA8 0BS. 01292 263488. No email. Web: www.gallowaydiocese.org.uk

Dundee	(St. Andrew).Cathedral House, 150 Nethergate, Dundee. DD1 4EA. 01382 225228/225453. email: enquiries@dunkelddiocese.org.uk web: www.standrewscathedral.co.uk
Edinburgh	(St. Mary Metropolitan). 61 York Place, Edinburgh EH1 3JD. 0131 5561798. email: cathedralhouse@stmaryscathedral.co.uk web: www.stmaryscathedral.co.uk
Glasgow	(St. Andrew). Clyde Street, Glasgow. G1 4JY. 0141 2213096. email: info@cathedralgl.org web: www.cathedralgl.org
Motherwell	(Our Lady of Good Aid). 31 Coursington Road, Motherwell.ML1 1PP. 01698 263045. email: info@motherwell-cathedral.org.uk web: www.motherwell-cathedral.org.uk
Oban	(St.Columba). Oban, Argyll. PA34 5AB. 01631 567436. email: editor@rcdai.org.uk web: www.rcdai.org.uk
Wales:	
Cardiff	(St. David), 38 Charles Street, Cardiff. CF10 2SF. 0292 0231407. email: cardiff.met.cath@btinternet.com web: cardiffmetropolitancathedral.org.uk
Swansea	(St. Joseph). Convent Street, Greenhill, Swansea. SA1 2BX. 01792 652683. email: pa@menevia.org web: stjosephscathedralswansea.org
Wrexham	(Our Lady of Sorrows). Regent Street, Wrexham. Clwyd. LL11 1RB. 01978 263943. No email. web: wrexhamcathedral.org.uk

COPTIC ORTHODOX CHURCH

(Archangel Michael and St. Anthony) of Egypt.

Stevenage	(St. George). Coptic Orthodox Church Centre, Shephall Manor, Stevenage. No email. web: www.copticcentre.com

GREEK ORTHODOX CATHEDRALS

It appears that in London there are several cathedrals in name, but the administration is at: (The Cathedral of the Dormition of the Mother of God). 22 Trinity Road, Wood Green, London N22 8LB. 02088882295. The only purpose-built cathedral is said to be:

London	(The Cathedral of the Divine Wisdom: St. Sophia) Moscow Road, London W2 4QW. 020 748 52149 For more details see the website: www.thyateira.org.uk
London	(All Saints) Camden Town, NW1 0JA. 020 77030137
London	(Nativity of the Mother of God) Camberwell. SE5 0TF.
London	(St. Andrew) Kentish Town, NW1 9QA. London (St. Nicholas) Shepherds Bush, W12 8JW.
London	(The Holy Cross and St. Michael) Golders Green, NW11 8DA.
Birmingham	(Dormition of the Mother of God and St. Andrew) 8 Arthur Place, Summerhill. Birmingham. B1 3DA
Glasgow	(St.Luke) 27 Dundonald Road, Dowanhill, Glasgow, G12 9LL. 0141 3397368. email:info@stluke.org.uk
Leicester	(St. Nicholas and St. Xenophon) Aylestone Road, Leicester. LE2 7LN

RUSSIAN ORTHODOX CATHEDRALS

London (The Dormition and All Saints)
Ennismore Gardens, SW7 1NH.

London (Dormition of the Most Holy Mother of
God and Holy Royal Martyrs)
57 Harvard Road, W4 4ED.

SERBIAN ORTHODOX CHURCH

London (St. Savas) Lancaster Road, W11 1QQ.

UKRAINIAN ORTHODOX CHURCH

London (London Cathedral) 1a Newton Avenue,
W3 8AJ.

OTHER DENOMINATIONS:

There are other churches listed as 'cathedrals' under the following titles, but information is difficult to achieve. Check with Wikipedia website: List of Cathedrals.

Ancient Catholic Church, Ancient and Old Catholic Church, Anglican Catholic Church, Church of England (Continuing), Free Church of England, Holy Catholic Church (Anglican Rite), Liberal Catholic Church, Traditional Church of England, Ukrainian Catholic Church (Exarchy of Great Britain).

APPENDIX B

Some notable architects connected with cathedrals.

Sir Christopher Wren (1632-1723) was an English scientist and mathematician and one of Britain's most distinguished architects, best known for the design of many London churches, including St. Paul's Cathedral. He was born on 20 October 1632 in East Knoyle, Wiltshire, where his father was rector. His father later moved to Windsor as chaplain to the King, and therefore he spent most of his formative years living in and around Windsor Castle where he was clearly influenced by its architecture. Wren was educated at Westminster School and then Oxford University. He showed an early talent for mathematics and enjoyed inventing things. In 1657, Wren was appointed professor of astronomy at Gresham College in London and four years later, professor of astronomy at Oxford. In 1662, he was one of the founding members of the Royal Society, along with other mathematicians, scientists and scholars, many of whom were his friends. Wren's interest in architecture developed from his study of physics and engineering. In 1664 and 1665, Wren was commissioned to design the Sheldonian Theatre in Oxford and a chapel for Pembroke College, Cambridge and from then on, architecture was his main focus. In 1665, Wren visited Paris, where he was strongly influenced by French and Italian Baroque styles and became intent on creating buildings similar to those seen on his travels.

On 2nd September 1666, the Great Fire of London destroyed much of the medieval city, providing a huge opportunity for Wren.

It is believed the King, Charles II, who had been a childhood friend, commissioned Wren to rebuild the destroyed city buildings. In 1669, he was appointed surveyor of the royal works which effectively gave him control of all government building in the country. He produced ambitious plans for rebuilding the whole area but they were rejected, partly because property owners insisted on keeping the sites of their destroyed buildings. Wren did design 51 new city churches, as well as the new St. Paul's Cathedral that took 35 years to complete when Wren was 60. He was knighted in 1673. In 1675, Wren was commissioned to design the Royal Observatory at Greenwich.

In 1682, he received another royal commission, to design a hospital in Chelsea for retired soldiers, and in 1696 a hospital for sailors in Greenwich. Other buildings include Trinity College Library in Cambridge and the facade of Hampton Court Palace. Wren often worked with the same team of craftsmen, including master plasterer John Groves and wood carver Grinling Gibbons.

Wren died on 25 February 1723 and was the first person to be buried in the cathedral.

George Gilbert Scott (1811-1878) started in architecture by designing gaols and workhouses, and later studied French Gothic cathedrals and churches, much influenced by the ideas of Augustus Welby Pugin. He represented High Victorian Gothic architecture, and was responsible for an immense amount of such work. Some of his best work is St. Giles' Church in Camberwell, the Albert Memorial in Kensington Gardens, the Midland Railway Terminus Hotel at St. Pancras and the Foreign Office in Whitehall, London. He was concerned with the creation, restoration and alteration of some 730 buildings and it is believed he designed 42 churches including St. John's College Cambridge. His restorations began with renovations of Ely Cathedral in 1847 and included Westminster Abbey (where he was made surveyor in 1849, and worked on the north front and the chapter house). He restored cathedrals of Chester, Chichester, Dundee St. Paul's, Durham (Tower), Edinburgh St. Mary's (Episcopal), Exeter, Glasgow St. Mary's, Gloucester, Hereford (incl. the famous Hereford Screen now in the V & A Museum), Oxford, Ripon, St. Albans, Wakefield, St. David's in Wales, and Lichfield (said to be his finest work). He was knighted in 1872 and is buried in Westminster Abbey. Two of his sons, George Gilbert Scott, Jr. and John Oldrid Scott, and his grandson Giles Gilbert Scott, became prominent architects.

Giles Gilbert Scott (1880-1960) was the third son of George Gilbert Scott junior (1839-97) and the grandson of Sir George Gilbert Scott. He was an English architect who designed numerous public buildings and like his famous grandfather, Sir George Gilbert Scott, was primarily a church builder – his greatest individual commission being for the new Liverpool Anglican Cathedral. The construction of this massive Gothic structure in red sandstone, begun in 1904, spanned Scott's entire working life and was completed only in 1980 by two of his associates. He had entered the second competition for the new Anglican Cathedral in Liverpool in 1902 with a *'Design for a Twentieth Century Cathedral'*. To his surprise, this was one of five designs chosen for a second round and in 1903 Scott's design was selected, but it was a choice which dismayed the Liverpool Cathedral Committee on account of Scott's age and lack of experience, and religion: he was still only 22 and a Roman Catholic.

A compromise was reached that George F. Bodley should join Scott as joint architect for the project. This joint collaboration was not a happy one, and indeed Scott was on the point of resignation when Bodley died in 1907 at which time the Lady chapel was unfinished. Scott promptly redesigned everything above the arcades, making the vault more elaborate and continental in style.

The first part of the cathedral was opened in 1910. In that same year the Cathedral Committee approved Scott's proposal to completely redesign the rest of the building, making his new conception much more monumental and, in its overall symmetry, almost Classical in feeling. Instead of twin towers inspired by Durham Cathedral, Scott now proposed a single, central tower rising above pairs of transepts which had the further advantage of providing the central space required. Described as a genius, he was knighted after the consecration ceremony in 1924. The building of Liverpool Cathedral, (see Further Reading) was an undertaking on a prodigious scale, and dominated Scott's life, but whilst he was feuding with Bodley in Liverpool, he managed to design his first complete church: the RC Church of the Annunciation in Bournemouth, in which he made a high transept similar to that he wanted at Liverpool.

Scott was noted for his blending of Gothic tradition with modernism, and his search for the 'middle line' in architecture caused him difficulties when he was appointed as architect for the new Coventry Cathedral in 1942. Pressured by the new Bishop of Coventry for a modern design and by the Royal Fine Arts Commission for a recreation of the old cathedral, he was criticised for trying to compromise between the two and designing a building that was neither fish nor fowl. Unable to reconcile these differences Scott resigned in 1947; a competition was held and won by Sir Basil Spence with an uncompromisingly modern design. Scott was responsible for many fine buildings including Battersea and Bankside Power Stations (the latter now the Modern Tate Gallery) and the iconic red telephone kiosks. During the First World War Scott was a major in the Royal Marines, and was in charge of building sea defences on the English Channel coast. His son, Richard Gilbert Scott, was also an architect. Giles Gilbert Scott died in 1960 and is buried with his wife outside the main entrance to Liverpool Cathedral; he can be seen in the bottom left of the Layman's window in the cathedral wearing a blue coat. Sadly he did not see the cathedral consecrated as this was delayed due to financial difficulties, and finally consecrated in 1978.

Basil Urwin Spence (1907-1976) was a Scottish architect, most notably associated with Coventry Cathedral and the Beehive (a wing of the New Zealand Parliament buildings) and also responsible for numerous other buildings in the Modernist style, including Edinburgh University Library, a power station in Wales, the British Embassy in Rome and the controversial Hyde Park Barracks. In 1939, Spence was commissioned as a 2nd lieutenant into the camouflage training and development unit of the British Army, and took part in the D-Day landings in 1944, reaching the rank of major and mentioned in despatches twice. During the war, Coventry's Anglican Cathedral had been almost completely destroyed by enemy bombing, and in 1944, Sir Giles Gilbert Scott had submitted a design proposal to rebuild the cathedral which was rejected by the Royal Fine Arts Commission. In 1950, a competition was launched to find the most suitable design, with over 200 entries submitted. Spence's radical design was ultimately chosen: work began in 1956 and the structure was completed in 1962. Spence was knighted in 1960 for his work at Coventry.

Augustus Welby Pugin (1812-1852) has been described as the foremost British architect of the 19th century, born in Bloomsbury, London. His father, Auguste, was a member of the French aristocracy who had fled France during the Revolution and it was from his father that he learned a love of medieval Gothic architecture. Augustus helped his father create a series of exact drawings providing details of medieval Gothic architecture and decoration. These drawings in such volumes as *Specimens of Gothic Architecture* (1821-3), and *Examples of Gothic Architecture* (1828-31), helped architects emulate Gothic style, and spawn the movement in architecture and design that is now called Victorian Gothic. So influential were the drawings that at the age of 19 he was employed to design furniture for Windsor Castle and had soon started his own business, carving architectural decoration in Gothic style.

Pugin had converted to Roman Catholicism, which filled him with a desire to express his faith through architecture. In support of his arguments in favour of authentic Gothic, Pugin produced his master work '*Contrasts*'; this and his subsequent works brought Pugin a number of architectural commissions, notably at Southwark Cathedral, and also St. Chad's RC Cathedral of Birmingham, St. Marie in Derby, and St. Oswald in Liverpool. One building stands perhaps above all others as a testament to his influence: the Palace of Westminster (Houses of Parliament) in London was built under the direction of Sir Charles Barry, but Pugin was responsible for every aspect of the interiors, as well as for working drawings of all the exterior details. In 1851 Pugin was working on the medieval court for the Great Exhibition (the Crystal Palace), but he suffered a breakdown from exhaustion and spent time in a private asylum before he finally died at his home in Ramsgate in 1852.

Pugin's influence extends beyond his own architectural designs. He was responsible for popularising a style of architecture that reached into every corner of Victorian life and influenced writers such as John Ruskin, and designers such as William Morris.

The appointment of an architect to all cathedrals is now essential and controlled by statute, with the main direction given below as an example:

Cathedrals Fabric Commission for England

ADVISORY NOTE 3 *Issued by the Commission April 1995 Revised December 2000*

THE SELECTION OF A CATHEDRAL ARCHITECT

Advice for Cathedral Chapters

1. The Statutory Requirements

1.1 The Cathedrals Measure 1999, Section 9(1)(f), requires the constitution of a Cathedral to "provide for the appointment of an architect", being a person registered under the Architects Act 1997. This provision replaces a similar requirement of the Cathedrals Measure 1963.

1.2 Under the Care of Cathedrals Measure 1990, Section 14(1) this architect ('the Cathedral Architect') has one specific statutory duty: in consultation with the Archaeological Consultant, to make a quinquennial report in writing "on works which he considers will need to be carried out as soon as practical in relation to the cathedral church and of the order in which he considers that they should be carried out". However in practice the Cathedral Architect will have a much wider range of duties (see The Role and Duties of the Cathedral Architect issued by the Cathedral Architects Association and the Cathedrals Fabric Commission).

1.3 The 1990 Measure, Section 12(1), requires the Administrative Body of a Cathedral (now the Chapter) to consult the Cathedrals Fabric Commission before appointing such a Cathedral Architect. This advice note sets out the general advice of the Commission on procedures that it believes will be helpful, and consideration of this advice by the Administrative Body will normally be regarded by the Commission as the first stage in such consultation.

1.4 Under the 1999 measure, Section 20, the Chapter of a Cathedral is also required to arrange for an architect or surveyor to carry out a quinquennial inspection of all other property (i.e., other than the Cathedral church) which the Chapter is liable to repair and maintain, and to report on the same. This provision replaces and changes a requirement of the Cathedrals Measure 1963.

An example of such a recent appointment is **Corinne Bennett** (1935 -2010) who was the first woman to be appointed as a cathedral architect in Britain. She spent the war years in Montreal and on return to England attended school knowing at age 12 that she wished to be involved with the repair of historic buildings. On leaving school in 1952 she studied at the Bartlett School of Architecture, part of University College London, graduating with a BA Hons in 1957. She first worked at Powell and Moya, and then in 1963 obtained a position with the Ministry of Public Buildings and Works, later to become English Heritage. After undertaking pioneering work in stone preservation with the Building Research Establishment she joined Purcell, Miller and Tritton as an associate and began work on repairs at

Ely Cathedral. She was appointed architect to the dean and chapter of Winchester in 1974 (until 1989) and directed the repairs to Winchester Cathedral for 15 years, where she arranged popular roof tours of the cathedral. Bennett's work included repairs to a substantial amount of stonework, especially the east end, over the chancel and the Lady chapel. She also restored the Rose window in the north transept and renewed much leadwork, conserved the misericords and choir seating, installed new internal and external lighting, and repaired some of the houses in the close. She was architect at Brighton Pavilion for 12 years and leading consultant for the restoration of the Albert Memorial in Hyde Park London. Her other work included Ealing Abbey, Mompesson House in Salisbury Close, Lacock Abbey and Mottisfont Abbey. Her most prized achievement was the reordering of the chapel of the English College in Rome. In 1991 she joined English Heritage as its national cathedrals architect and then was representative to the Church of England's Cathedral Fabric Commission in 1966 until 2006. Her architectural independence, clarity of thought and vast experience ensured her advice at many site visits. Later she chaired the fabric committee of St. George's Cathedral, Southwark. Corinne Bennett was appointed MBE in 1988 mainly for her conservation work on churches in Kent.

APPENDIX C

DISCIPLES & APOSTLES

The terms are sometimes interchanged. In the Bible, the Gospels and the Book of Acts refer to varying numbers of disciples that range from 70 to a "growing multitude". In the Book of Acts, the apostles themselves have disciples. The word 'disciple' is reported to appear 232 times in the four gospels and the Book of Acts. Jesus' inner circle of 12 disciples probably corresponds to the 12 tribes of Israel. Some names are more famous than others: the gospels name Peter as the first among the disciples, the first to name Jesus the messiah, on whom the church is built. Thomas, for example, is associated with a saying as 'doubting Thomas'. Judas was apparently designated to keep account of the 'money bag' but is best known for his role in betraying Jesus into the hands of the Roman authorities. Jesus is said to have appointed the disciples and sent them out in pairs on a specific mission, as in the gospel of Mark where Jesus sent out the 12 in pairs, to towns in Galilee with their initial instructions to heal the sick and drive out demons, and in the gospel of Matthew to raise the dead, but some scholars read this more imaginatively as instructions to heal the spiritually sick and thus to drive away wicked behaviour. They are also instructed to *"take nothing for their journey, except a staff only: no bread, no wallet, no money in their purse, but to wear sandals, and not put on two tunics".* Their carrying of just a staff (Matthew and Luke say not even a staff) is sometimes given as the reason for the use by Christian bishops of a staff of office.

The 12 Disciples of Jesus were brave men, for nearly all met violent deaths for their beliefs and actions. Although the four gospels give slightly differing accounts, according to tradition they were:

Peter: renamed by Jesus to Peter (meaning rock), his original name was Simon bar Jonah and he was a fisherman from Bethsaida of Galilee, also known as Simon bar Jochanan, Cephas and Simon Peter; thus a Galilean fisherman given a leadership role, described as 'first' among the disciples, but after his arrest denied knowing Jesus three times. He is associated with the foundation of the Church in Rome.

Andrew: brother of Simon/Peter and also a Galilean fisherman, said to have been a former disciple of John the Baptist, who travelled to the Mount of Olives with Jesus and was martyred by crucifixion at Patras in Greece.

Bartholomew: took Christianity to Armenia, was flayed and then crucified. He is now Patron of butchers, Florentine cheese merchants, and also nervous diseases.

James: son of Zebedee, brother of John: one of the first disciples to join Jesus, and known as James the Greater. He took Christianity to Spain, and is believed to have been beheaded in Judea (now Israel) although his body 'sailed' to Spain.

James: son of Alphaeus, known as James the Lesser or James the Just: was sentenced to death and martyred in Egypt with his body sawn into pieces.

John: brother of James, also a Galilean fisherman and an earlier disciple of John the Baptist. Jesus named both of them 'Bo-aner'ges', which means 'sons of thunder'. He prepared the Last Supper with Peter and sat then next to Jesus. He was imprisoned and died in Ephesus (Asia Minor now Turkey).

Judas: sometimes known as Judas Iscariot (perhaps referring to a town), the son of Simon, he betrayed Jesus for a bribe of 30 pieces of silver. A controversial gospel of Judas published in 2006 implied he was the chosen disciple and had been stoned to death by the others for his sin. He was replaced by Matthias as an apostle shortly after Jesus' resurrection.

Jude: patron saint of desperate cases and lost causes. Also known as Thaddeus. He preached the gospel in Judea, Syria, Mesopotamia (now Iraq) and Libya, and was axed to death in Persia (Iran).

Matthew: the tax collector who wrote one of the four gospels. He might also have been called Levi, and died in Ethiopia.

Philip: preached in Greece and Syria, before being crucified upside down.

Simon the Zealot: sometimes identified as Simeon of Jerusalem. After evangelising in Egypt he went to Persia and Armenia, and is said to have visited Britain. He was martyred by being sawn into pieces.

Thomas: doubted that Jesus had risen from the dead and demanded to feel the wounds before believing. Also known as Judas Thomas, being a 'twin'. He travelled to India and died in Madras.

The apostles are portrayed in the New Testament as having been Galilean Jews, and this is supported in several ways. The names of the majority of them are Hebrew names, although some had Greek names; Jesus' statements that his mission was directed only to those of the house of Israel implies that the 12 'apostles' and others closest to Jesus were all Jews, as does the fact that only after the death of Jesus did the apostles agree apparently with Paul that the teaching of the gospel could be extended to others, especially 'uncircumcised gentiles'. The Book of Acts recounts the deeds of the apostles in the years after Jesus' crucifixion. Saint Paul claimed the role of apostle to the gentiles and, assuming Peter's role, became apostle to the Jews. Paul did not restrict the term apostle to the 12, either because he didn't know it or resisted it. In Western Christianity it is usual to refer to them as disciples while in Eastern Christianity they are usually referred to as apostles. Using the original Greek words, both titles are descriptive as an *apostle* is one sent on a mission whereas a disciple is a student. In more modern usage, major missionaries are sometimes termed apostles, as in Saint Patrick, Apostle of Ireland.

The word *disciple* is used today usually as a method of identification for those who seek to learn from the teachings of Jesus.

APPENDIX D

THE REFORMATION (and the Civil Wars).

Cathedrals and churches probably suffered more harm and damage during these two 'wars' than at any time so it is well to understand something of the background. A most unusual quotation, to reflect upon now, on Protestantism comes from Martin Luther (1520): *"If you think properly of the gospel, please do not imagine that its cause can be advanced without tumult, offence and sedition... the word of God is a sword, it's war, ruin, offence, perdition and poison. If I am immoderate, at least I am simple and open."*

We have to remember that the 16th century was the time of the Reformation in Europe – a religious conflict between Protestants and Catholics that divided Western Europe for over 150 years – and at a time in Britain when there was internal warfare not always involving the Church, but certainly at times the bishops and other officials and supporters were involved. The Reformation is said to have started with a protest in 1517 when Martin Luther, a German monk of Augustinian practice, nailed his 95 theses to a church in Wittenberg. These spiritual doubts of one monk grew into a religious movement known as 'Protestantism', named after Luther's protest. He was a gifted scholar and wished to return to the text of the Bible and reject current practices for which he could not account in the Bible. It is interesting and challenging to read some of Martin Luther's beliefs and challenges about the Catholic Church then:

That people could not 'buy off' their sins by paying money to the Church, only god could pardon sins, not the Church; that people were naturally sinful and that they should seek salvation by believing in God, making pilgrimages to holy places and by doing good works; that priests should be subject to the law of the land in the same way as ordinary men and women; that priests were not divine beings; that all people should be allowed to read the Bible, not just priests – the Catholic Church believed that if all people were allowed to read the Bible they would form their own opinions and that the Bible would become more important than the Church; that the Church should not display rich images of saints and crucifixes and that priests should not wear elaborate clothing: that priests did not have the power to turn the bread and wine into the body and blood of Christ during Communion.

Specifically he rejected the authority of the Pope in Rome and such an action usually led to a charge of heresy and burning at the stake. However, he was supported by various German princes and because of the printing press was able to propagate his theories that encouraged religious conflict and rebellion throughout Christendom. In England Henry VIII converted to Protestantism forcing most of the nation with him.

The Reformation in England

In 1527 Henry VIII wrote a book entitled 'Fidei Defensor' that criticised Martin Luther and confirmed the status of the Pope. However, just six years later in 1533, Henry passed legislation that removed the Pope's influence in England and made himself the Head of the Church of England. The King began to have doubts about the validity of his marriage to Catherine of Aragon. In the 18 years that they had been married she had given birth to eight children but only one had survived, a girl, Mary. Henry believed that his lack of male heir to the throne was God's way of punishing him for having married his brother's wife, as he had found a passage in the Bible that supported his belief. Henry had also become infatuated with Anne Boleyn and so asked Catherine to grant him a divorce but she refused. According to the law in England only the Pope could grant a king a divorce. But after five years of waiting Henry began to take matters into his own hands.

In 1532 all bishops were forced to sign a document stating that they would make no new laws without the consent of the king, and that Church officials would not meet without the approval of the king. An Act was passed that stopped the English Church from sending money to Rome. Thomas Cranmer, who believed that the king should be head of the Church, was appointed as Archbishop of Canterbury – the highest and most influential church position in England. Cranmer became famous for his important tasks as the co-author and editor of the first and second Books of Common Prayer. In 1533 Anne Boleyn became pregnant: the king secretly married her and declared his marriage to Catherine to have been invalid. The 'Act in Restraint of Appeals' was passed that made it illegal for any foreigner to interfere in English law or to have more authority in England than the King. In 1534 an Act was passed that transferred all church monies that would be normally sent to Rome to the King. It also declared Henry to be the only Supreme Head on Earth of the Church of England. The Act of Succession was also passed, removing Mary from the line of succession and granting succession to the children of his relationship with Anne Boleyn. The Act also contained a clause that would allow Henry to force everyone in the land to swear an oath recognising the terms of the Act: anyone refusing to take the oath would be guilty of treason. Both John Fisher and Thomas More (leaders of political resistance to the laws) refused to swear the oath and both men were executed.

In 1534 the Act of Supremacy was passed, declaring England as a sovereign state with the King as head of both the country and the Church. It gave Henry the power to reform the church as he saw fit and also to appoint churchmen of his own choosing. 1536 saw 'The Act against the Pope's Authority' that removed the last traces of papal power in England, including the Pope's right to decide disputed points of Scripture: the passing of this Act, together with the Act in Restraint of Appeals (1533) and the Act of Supremacy (1534) made it unacceptable for monastic communities, who owed allegiance to parent institutions outside England, to remain.

By 1536 all monasteries in England were closed, their gold and riches claimed by the King and the land given to loyal nobles. The break with Rome was not the absolute

Reformation; it was more the assembling and spreading of ideas that caused reform. After the Reformation Holy Communion replaced the Catholic Mass, and elaborate crosses and crucifixes were forbidden. The structure and theology of the Church was a matter of fierce dispute for generations. These disputes were finally ended by a coup d'état in 1688, from which emerged an established Church and a number of non-conformist Churches whose members at first suffered various civil limitations which were only removed over time, as did the substantial minority who remained Roman Catholic in England and Wales, whose organisation remained illegal until the 19th century. (For an excellent and more thorough readable account of the Reformation see the entry 'The English Reformation' on the Wikepedia website.)

In Scotland James V was in need of money to support his court and tried to persuade the Pope to grant tax concessions by appearing to support Protestantism. He had tried, unsuccessfully, to ban distribution of the books and their message. When the Lutheran books appeared in print, the radical message made a strong impression on the Scots and notably one John Knox, a fiery preacher in Edinburgh. James V died in 1542 and Scotland faced a more severe crisis with his heir, the Catholic Queen Mary. Religion was very important to the Scots in the 16th century – particularly in a social sense, as the Church was responsible for education, health, and welfare, and also the 'discipline' of the nation. To state it bluntly, one's future in heaven or in hell was at stake. Early in this century Scotland, perhaps more than England, could be said to be a 'Catholic' nation, but its people, becoming increasingly educated, sought personal ideas and experience of spiritual experience with ideas of reform rather than just following Rome.

This 'Reformation' split the Church into Catholic and Protestant, creating the two roads to salvation – both claiming to be true – and a break with Rome. France and England were involved in attempting to control the Scottish throne by 'wedding' Mary: England was now Protestant, France was mainly Catholic. The power struggle spread unfortunately, yet again, not by religious denomination or domination, but into war. The period then became known as 'Rough Wooing' when England tried to force Mary's hand through invasion and the French even supplied the Scots with troops and arms. All sides spent a fortune on this rough wooing of the Scots and it is said that King Henry VIII of England wasted the fortune he had made from his dissolution of the monasteries in England on his campaigns. Protestantism was here to stay in various forms with, in Scotland, a new established Church.

The Civil War of England (1642-1649) is one of the most remarkable and important events in the history of England. The monarchy and the people were in open conflict for the first time: a conflict that became a religious and a political war. The Puritans, led by Oliver Cromwell, and the Parliament united against the King – Charles – and condemned his interference in religious affairs. The King did not care for the existence of either: the Parliament along with the Puritans combined to dispute the King's authority to lay down the law in Church and State. The main issue at stake was whether sovereignty resided in the King alone, or whether both the King and Parliament should share power. This discontent broke out into a struggle between King Charles, on the one hand, and Parliament on the other, and came to be known as the English Civil War or the Puritan Revolution.

In addition, 'bishops' wars' had been fought between the Scots and English forces led by Charles I that paved the way for the uprising of Parliament that began the English civil wars. Charles had been attempting to enforce Anglican reforms onto the Scottish Church that was opposed to this, and even wanted to destroy the control that bishops had over the Church. Charles' proposed reforms were rejected by the Scottish Assembly at Glasgow in 1638. He was furious that the Scots had rejected his proposals, and hastily formed an English force with which to march on Scotland in 1639 but did not have the funds for such a military expedition, nor confidence in his troops, so he was forced to leave Scotland without fighting a battle. The unrest continued in Scotland, and when Charles discovered that they had been plotting with the French he again decided to mount a military expedition. This time, Charles called Parliament in order to get funds (1640) but members wanted to discuss grievances against the government, and were opposed to any military operation. This angered Charles and he dismissed Parliament again, hence the name 'Short Parliament' that it is commonly called. Charles went ahead with his military operation without Parliament's support, and was beaten by the Scots who, taking advantage of this, went on to seize Northumberland and Durham. Charles found himself in a desperate position, and was forced to call Parliament again in November, 1640. This Parliament is known as the 'Long Parliament'.

The tension between Charles and Parliament was great, since none of the issues raised by the Short Parliament had been resolved. This tension was brought to a head on January 4th, 1642, when Charles attempted to arrest five members of Parliament. This attempt failed, since they were spirited away before the King's troops arrived. Charles left London and both he and Parliament began to stockpile military resources and recruit troops. Charles officially began the war by raising his standard at Nottingham in August, 1642. At this stage of the wars, Parliament had no wish to kill the King. It was hoped that Charles could be reinstated as ruler, but with a more constructive attitude to Parliament. The majority of the country was neutral in the civil wars, and both sides only had about 13,000 men in 1642. The areas of Royalist support tended to be the North, West and Wales. Parliamentarians were supported by the richer South and East, including London. Parliament also held most of the ports, since the merchants that ran them saw more profit in a Parliament-led country.

The first war stretched from 1642 to 1646. Charles marched on London, hoping for a quick victory that would negate the benefits of Parliament's resources, but was soon forced to withdraw to Oxford, where his headquarters was based for the rest of the war. In 1643, many battles were fought all over the country and after the testing of the major armies, both sides sought allies elsewhere.

Parliament drew up the 'Solemn League & Covenant', which promised the Scots religious reforms in return for their help. Charles negotiated a ceasefire in Ireland that freed English troops for action on the mainland. Eventually the 'New Model Army' was formed and won two important victories, effectively destroying all of Charles' armies. In 1646, Charles had little choice but to disband his remaining forces. Oxford surrendered, and Charles fled north seeking refuge with the Scots, bringing the first war to a close. Charles was ransomed by Parliament, and held at Holmby House whilst Parliament drew up proposals, and began to disband its army. However, the army was unhappy about issues such as arrears of pay and living conditions, and resisted the disbandment. Eventually the army kidnapped Charles in an attempt to win a bargaining piece but Charles escaped to the Isle of Wight. The army marched to London and debated its own proposals. Charles took advantage of this shift of emphasis away from him to negotiate a new agreement with the Scots, again promising Church reform (28th Dec 1647).

This agreement led to the second war. A series of royalist rebellions and a Scottish invasion (July 1648) took place. However, all were defeated by the now powerful standing army. This new betrayal by Charles caused Parliament to debate whether Charles should be returned to power at all and those who still supported Charles' throne tried once more to negotiate with him.

The army, angry that Parliament was still considering Charles as a ruler, marched on Parliament where 45 MPs were arrested, 146 were kept out of Parliament, and only

75 were allowed in, and then only to do the army's bidding. This 'rump Parliament' was ordered to set up a high court of justice in order to try Charles I for treason in the name of the people of England. The trial of the King found Charles guilty as charged, and he was beheaded on January 30th. Cromwell then led the army in quelling revolts in Ireland and Scotland (1649-50) to finally restore an uneasy peace. Charles II claimed the throne and was crowned in Scotland. He marched then with the Scots on England. Cromwell beat the Scottish forces at Dunbar but could not prevent Charles II marching deep into England. During this period many churches and cathedrals were used by the rival armies as hostels and even stables, and much damage was caused to permanent artefacts that could not be hidden. Cromwell finally engaged and beat the new king at Worcester on 3rd September 1651. Charles II fled abroad, ending the civil wars. 'The Commonwealth' was then established, with Oliver Cromwell as Lord Protector of England. The following 18th century was, perhaps surprisingly, one of more unison in Britain, with warfare moving to Europe and Americas, and with trade, overseas and at home, becoming an important and influential aspect of life in the whole of Britain, leading to the Renaissance. The Churches had learned from the strong and wise words of Luther and Knox and became ever more active, until the post-war periods following the two World Wars saw a decline in beliefs and attendance at most churches.